Unthinkable

REAL ANSWERS FOR FAMILIES

CONFRONTING CATASTROPHIC

INJURY OR DEATH

Unthinkable

REAL ANSWERS FOR FAMILIES

CONFRONTING CATASTROPHIC

INJURY OR DEATH

J. KYLE BACHUS, ESQ.

LIONCREST
PUBLISHING

UNTHINKABLE

Real Answers For Families Confronting Catastrophic Injury or Death

ISBN	978-1-5445-2795-6	*Hardcover*
	978-1-5445-2794-9	*Paperback*
	978-1-5445-2796-3	*Ebook*

Mom, more than thirty years ago, you enthusiastically encouraged my dreams of becoming a lawyer.

What we didn't know was that my most meaningful case would involve your wrongful death.

We all miss you so much!

Contents

The Call No One Wants to Get

It was eight in the evening, Denver time, on Wednesday, April 28, 2020. Our COVID-19 lives were just beginning. I had finished a workout in the basement and was sitting in the kitchen eating a barbecue sandwich when my phone rang.

My sister, in Florida—calling at ten o'clock her time? That didn't happen very often. I answered.

"Kyle?"

"Hey…"

She wasn't crying, but I could tell something was wrong. "The Winter Park police just left my house," she said.

My sister lived in a suburb of Orlando, not in Winter Park, which is about thirty miles away. But our mother lived in Winter Park.

"Is it Mom?" I asked.

We are a close family; before COVID-19, my mother watched my sister's kids in the afternoons. My mother and I had spoken just the day before, preparing to put her house on the market.

"Yes," my sister said.

"Something happened to her." It wasn't a question. I already knew the answer.

"Yes."

"Is she dead?" I knew the answer to that too. My sister hadn't begun by saying she was on the way to the hospital. She hadn't started with, *There's been an accident, but Mom's okay.*

"Yes."

My sister told me the officer had knocked on her door, asked if Margaret Bachus was her mother, and told her our mom had been hit and killed by a car while she was out on her walk that evening. Daily walks were my mother's way of staying active during COVID-19. The officer handed my sister a card with her direct dial number, offered her condolences, and asked if my sister was okay. And then, with that, the officer left.

You might think I'd have been prepared for a call like that. I graduated from the University of Florida law school in 1992 and started work for a personal injury law firm the next Monday. My childhood love of reading had led me to the law, and my affinity for the underdog led me to the *David vs. Goliath* world of personal injury law, first in Florida and then in Colorado. I co-founded a firm in Denver in 1996 that has expanded to thirty lawyers and about one hundred staff in four offices. At the time of my mother's death, I had twenty-eight years of experience in the field. In that time, I had handled hundreds of cases involving catastrophic injuries and worked with more than one hundred families who had suffered the loss of a close family member. I've had as many as a dozen cases involving other families in situations similar to ours at the same time.

But there is no preparing for such a call. There's no way to be ready for that knock on the door. In an instant, everything is different and will be from that moment on. It's impossible to grasp the impact of an event like this unless you've experienced it yourself. The only way I can describe my mindset in the moments after I learned of my mother's death is shock. My older brother and younger sister are both doctors, and they're also familiar with death and tragedy through their work; we were all left reeling.

For all of us, nothing would be the same again.

I walked upstairs to tell my wife and could hear the kids in their rooms nearby. "My sister just called," I began. "My mom was killed tonight, out on her walk. She was hit and killed by a car."

My wife burst into tears. "What?! Are you sure?" she asked.

The kids came at the sound of their mother crying. At the time, my daughter was fifteen, and our sons were twelve and ten. Everyone in the family called my mother "Big Sissy" because she was an older sister herself and that's just the kind of person she was.

"Big Sissy is dead," I told my kids. And, with that, their lives changed forever too.

MOVING BEYOND SHOCK

You may be reading this book because someone you love has been killed or catastrophically injured too. You've gotten the call or the knock on the door, and you're reeling, just like my family. We all walk through our days aware that terrible things happen to other people, but we don't expect them to happen to us. It's a defense mechanism; without it, we'd be paralyzed, unable to move through life, spending our days locked up at home for safety.

But terrible things can happen to me, to you, to anyone else at any moment. And if you *do* find yourself in a situation like this, guidance on what comes next and how to respond is difficult to come by. So is regaining some sense of control in a world that's suddenly whirling.

I'm sorry for the loss you've suffered and the pain you're feeling in this moment. I can't wipe them away. Believe me, I would if I could.

But what I can do, through this book, is walk alongside you. I can draw on my decades of experience as a personal injury lawyer as well as the personal experience of my mother's death to provide you with a path of knowledge to travel.

ARE YOU A PROFESSIONAL IN THE FIELD?

I've written this book with you in mind too, in hopes that it will prove useful to you, your colleagues, and the families you work with. Thank you for your work.

The chapters in this book are arranged in roughly the order in which issues are likely to arise following the unexpected death or injury of a loved one. In Part 1, we'll discuss what you need to know about dealing with the police and their investigation. We'll cover the possibility of a criminal prosecution and why families are so often disappointed in the outcome. I'll address victims' rights and what they might mean for you.

In Parts 2 and 3, we'll talk about the many practical matters you'll need to handle, whether your loved one has died or suffered a life-altering injury—quickly, during a time when it's so difficult to even think straight, when you don't feel capable of anything more than simply hanging on.

In Part 4, we'll talk about seeking accountability and what bringing a civil case against a company or an individual who may be responsible for your loss can and can't accomplish. We'll talk about the importance of seeking help to manage your grief and the resources available to pay for it. And we'll address legacy: the hope of finding meaning of some kind in the tragedy you've experienced.

If you've experienced the sudden death of a loved one, Parts 1, 2, and 4 are most relevant to you. If a loved one has suffered a catastrophic injury, then you will find Parts 1, 3, and 4 most relevant. But that's not to say that you shouldn't read it all if you choose to; I hope you'll find useful information throughout.

Whether your loved one has died or suffered a catastrophic injury, you've gotten the call no one wants to get. I have too. You have questions, many of them pressing, and you need answers. You fear making mistakes because their consequences could last forever.

Your life has changed forever too—but it *does* and *must* go on. I'm writing this book because I want to help by sharing what I've learned about these topics through my work, representing people like you, and what I've learned through the shattering experience of my mother's death. I can't think of a better way of honoring Big Sissy than that.

A COMPANION WEBSITE

I've created a companion website, KyleBachus.com, where you can find supporting material related to the book. I'll point you to the website in the text in instances where you may find it useful.

PART I

The Investigation and the Criminal Justice System

Two legal systems come into play in the aftermath of a catastrophic death or injury: the criminal justice system and the civil justice system. They serve different purposes, operate by different rules, and lead to different results.

The criminal justice system is there to enforce society's rules. By bringing a criminal case, the government holds a wrongdoer accountable for actions that society has defined as a crime that deserves punishment. A family that has suffered a traumatic loss or a catastrophic injury can't decide to bring a criminal case; only the police or a prosecutor who works for the government can do that. The purpose of a criminal case isn't making the family whole, although it can result in limited restitution for expenses you've incurred.

Bottom line: the criminal justice system exists to protect society by upholding our legal standards of right and wrong.

The civil justice system, on the other hand, is about seeking compensation for loss. The government can bring a civil case, but that's not what we're talking about here. If the person harmed was a private individual, only they, their family, or in some cases, their insurance company can bring a civil case. Civil cases are handled by a private lawyer, and the result can't involve jail time, only money.

Criminal justice is in the hands of the government, although the family has rights and a role it can play. Civil justice is different; it's typically in the hands of the family.

I'll talk about the civil justice system in detail in Part 4. I'm covering criminal justice first because a criminal case, if there is one, typically comes first.

CHAPTER 1

The Investigation

Broadly speaking, the law enforcement officers I've encountered want to do a great job, just as anyone else who cares about their work does. And when an incident results in a death or catastrophic injury, law enforcement officers are usually among the first people summoned to assist. But as with anyone else, their ability to do a great job is bounded by their training, their experience, and the nature of their responsibilities. And that is why I say that depending on the police alone to investigate a fatal or catastrophic incident involving your loved one amounts to playing the lottery.

The police officer who came to my sister's house told her that our mother had been hit and killed by a car. The next day, we began to suspect that might not be exactly the case, and two days later, we knew it for sure. The truth began to emerge only by chance: one of our neighbors in Denver had a friend in Winter Park, Florida, who called her attention to a social media post about a pedestrian who had been hit and killed by a concrete mixer truck there.

The fact that a concrete mixer truck was responsible for my mother's death wasn't the only thing we determined on our own.

There was also the specific location where my mom was killed: a busy intersection not far from her home in Winter Park. And the time of day too: at 4:50 p.m., about five hours before my sister was notified.

When I got the Winter Park police officer on the phone the day after my mom was killed and asked for more information, she told me the incident remained under investigation. It would be another day or so, she said, before they would be ready to sit down with us.

My purpose in sharing this is not to fault the Winter Park police. When we did meet, they told us they had withheld the fact that a concrete mixer truck was involved because they didn't want to make the tragedy of our loss any harder to bear. Like anyone else, they were trying to do a great job.

But for the family of the victim, there's anguish in not knowing. Learning as much information as soon as possible about the *how* and *why* can be very important to family members after a tragedy happens. And that is not the only consequence, especially if the other party involved is a commercial entity, like a trucking company. The evidence you will need to hold them accountable is fleeting, and you can't always count on the police to gather it for you. What's more, the commercial entity probably understands the fleeting nature of evidence too and can be quick to gather it in order to protect its own interests.

Immediately after calling the police, the driver of the truck that killed my mother did what he was supposed to do. He reported the accident to the dispatcher or a safety officer at his company, which happened to be one of the largest concrete truck operators in the United States. As it happened, the driver had just finished dropping concrete at a major construction site served by multiple trucks about three blocks from where my mom was killed. Within an hour, if not sooner, the company had its own representative on the scene—and the police were no longer the only ones talking to witnesses and gathering evidence. And of course, it would be hours before my family was even notified, and days before the police told us that a commercial truck was involved.

We were fortunate in this one respect: because of the work I do, I knew the consequences of relying entirely on the police and their investigation. Thankfully, my law partner took responsibility for finding our own answers, leaving me to focus on my family. He reached out immediately to law firms in Florida we'd worked with before and got in touch with an accident reconstruction engineer and a private investigator they recommended, who headed directly to Winter Park.

THE RANDOMNESS OF THE POLICE RESPONSE

If something bad happens to a loved one in New York City, the investigation is probably going to be led by a detective or specialist with considerable experience, simply because of where it happened. If the same event occurs in a rural area or a small town, you may find there are only a handful of officers on duty and that the one who's sent out to start securing evidence at the scene has never done it before, or has done it as infrequently as once a year. It's not the fault of the law enforcement officers. That's just the reality of the situation. Some departments share jurisdiction and can call on state police or highway patrol officers who have more experience. But the lead investigator within a particular department in the event of a catastrophic death or injury is most likely going to be determined by who happens to be on duty when the event occurs. That is why I say it's a lottery.

THE FLEETING NATURE OF EVIDENCE

You could slip on a sidewalk and suffer a serious injury—or even be killed—but typically in our society the most severe accidents involve motor vehicles. And when a crash occurs, there's physical evidence left that can tell the story of what happened. It's right there on the roadway: the position of the vehicles, skid marks, debris, lane markings, traffic lights, and the condition of the road in the weather. That is why the police close the roadway right away: to secure the scene and the evidence to be found there. And from the moment the event occurs, that evidence begins to dissipate. Time is of the essence.

The first thing investigators try to determine is where the impact occurred. They're looking at crush damage, the position of vehicles and debris. Then, they want to back up in time. Where were the vehicles a half-second before impact? One second? Three? Five? What can skid marks tell them about how fast a vehicle was going and whether the driver tried to stop? All of this is reconstructed through an accident investigation with the help of technology, and there's nothing automatic or infallible about it. If investigators get the point of impact wrong, then the rest of the data may be wrong.

Why would evidence dissipate? Consider the weather. Is the road wet? Is it snowing and slippery? Beyond weather, the biggest impact on physical evidence comes when the police open the road again. Streets have to function; traffic needs to flow; we've all got places to go. The police need to gather the evidence they need as quickly as they can, so they can reopen the road.

Witnesses are often the first to reach the driver and ask if they're okay and what happened; that makes what the driver told them important. If it's an at-fault driver in a catastrophic accident, what they say initially may be very different than what they tell the police who arrive in a patrol car three, five, or ten minutes later. And witnesses won't linger at the scene forever. Some will walk away without even giving their names, never mind a statement.

These days, data evidence is very important. Many intersections have cameras; so do businesses and residential doorbells, Uber drivers, and taxis. All these cameras have limited storage, and eventually, they'll record over themselves, whether it's in one day or fifteen. If the footage isn't secured in that time, the video is lost forever. Vehicles now carry the equivalent of black boxes, called ECMs, that are constantly recording variables such as speed, braking, and airbag deployment. They may capture the last fifteen or twenty seconds before an accident occurs—but once the vehicle drives off, that data can be overridden too. Some police departments may not know how to download the data; how this is done can vary from vehicle to vehicle.

In our case, the concrete truck company told the police not to worry, that they would take the vehicle, park it, and download the black box data. Maybe that was fine—but I was certainly concerned when I learned it. You'd prefer that the police impound the vehicle and tow it away themselves to secure any evidence, but they may not.

GOALS AND INTENTIONS

It's also important to understand that everyone involved in an investigation does not share the same goals and intentions.

If the victim is dead, of course, they can't speak for themselves, and the same may be true if they're catastrophically injured. And of course, there's always the possibility that the police will determine your loved one was at fault.

The police are trying to determine fault—and whether a crime has been committed. That means they're asking a specific set of questions, based on the circumstances and the criminal laws that the police are empowered to enforce. Their responsibility is to protect the interests of society at large, not those of the individual victim.

The person who caused the event is likely to recognize that they're in jeopardy and act out of self-preservation. We might like to think they'd admit they're at fault and responsible, but that just doesn't happen very often.

Again, that is especially true if the other party is a commercial entity. In the event of a crash, the goal of a sophisticated company is limiting financial consequences to owners and shareholders. You probably have no plan in place for coping with the unexpected because it's unexpected. But large commercial trucking and fleet owners know that accidents are foreseeable. Drive enough miles, and accidents *will* happen. So, these companies, and their insurance companies, have plans in place to put teams of people on the ground immediately if they need to. While you're still stunned and trying to figure out the basics of what happened, they're actively working to protect their interests.

CHOICES THE POLICE COULD MAKE

Upon completing their investigation, the choices that the police officers can make range from taking no action to writing a traffic ticket to bringing more significant criminal charges. Prosecutors might decide to add or drop charges later, but it's typically the police who start the process.

For police investigators, the decision about whether to file significant criminal charges usually comes down to the question of intent. Legally, it's called *mens rea*, a Latin term. If someone who has been drinking and driving gets behind the wheel and causes a crash that harms or kills someone else, the police can bring significant criminal charges because they can demonstrate criminal intent. That is because the law presumes that if you drink and drive, you knew that what you were doing was likely to cause harm to others.

But if someone takes their eyes off the roadway ahead for a moment and accidentally runs a red light and causes a similar crash , they may face nothing more than a low-level traffic ticket. In both cases, someone is left dead or badly injured. But in the case of accidentally running a red light, the police may find no evidence to suggest the driver actually *intended* to harm others. The police may conclude the driver simply made a mistake with tragic results. The consequences of a low-level, "careless driving resulting in serious injury or death" ticket issued to a driver can be terribly out of proportion to the magnitude of the harm caused—but under the law, the police may determine it's all that's warranted.

If you conduct a deep enough investigation, you'll typically find there's a reason why the crash occurred. Maybe the driver's foot slipped off the brake pedal. They might have been on their cell phone. In commercial trucking cases, you might find that the driver has been at the wheel longer than regulations permit; they're beyond the hours and fatigued. The traffic flow at a busy intersection could be confusing to a driver from out of town.

Finding a reason for an accident, and even determining who's responsible for it, is not the same as establishing criminal intent. A driver might be careless—negligent, in legal terms, meaning they failed to do what a reasonable person would do in those circumstances—but that doesn't necessarily mean they committed a serious crime under the law in your state.

The legal fine points are endless. Intentionally running a red light and bombing through an intersection at sixty miles per hour is much different under criminal law than accidentally running a red light. If you're texting while you're driving and cause a crash, that suggests you're consciously disregarding the safety of others and may face significant criminal charges. Accidentally failing to brake in time and rear-ending the car in front of you is negligent, but you almost never go to jail for mere negligence. That doesn't mean there's no accountability for negligence; we'll get to that later, in our discussion about civil lawsuits. It does mean that negligence itself is not generally considered to be a serious crime.

MAKING YOUR CASE A PRIORITY FOR THE POLICE

In our society, we view the police as authority figures, and appropriately so. But they are public servants. They work as employees within the structure of a town or city government. In some ways, they're inescapably political, and we have access to them just as we do other public employees. That also means that, as the saying goes, the squeaky wheel gets the grease.

As was the case with my family, your initial connection to the police is likely to be the business card of the officer or investigator who notified you of the accident. You're also entitled to know the hierarchy of the department: the names and positions of the other people involved in the investigation and the roles they play. Depending on the size of the department, you might find that behind the traffic officer who responded to the scene is a higher-level investigator of some kind, such as a fatality investigator or an accident reconstructionist. Above them you might find the police chief. It is completely appropriate for you to say that you'd like to speak to the highest-ranking officer involved, just to be sure you have a good understanding of how your particular case is going to unfold. Once I understood the hierarchy of the Winter Park police—a small department in a small city with limited experience investigating traffic fatalities—I called and asked them to schedule a meeting, so I could introduce myself to the chief.

The goal in all this is to make the police aware at the highest level that their investigation is extremely important to your family and that you're monitoring their progress. Why? Because police departments get very busy. And it's just a fact of human nature, whether you're talking about a dry cleaner or a police investigator: the more the people you're dealing with understand that you're actively involved and that this matters deeply to you, the better the chances you're going to get the highest quality of work in the most timely fashion. When your family has suffered a traumatic loss, there may be no greater priority for you than getting to the bottom of what happened, why it happened, and making sure that the people involved are held accountable, not only for your family's sake, but to make sure that it doesn't happen again to someone else. So, bring a picture of your loved one or their children to your meeting with the police. Tell them about the importance to you of the person you've lost or who's been injured, make clear you want to do anything you can to encourage and assist them, and tell them how thankful you are for the work they're doing.

Although it is unlikely, you might encounter a defensive reaction, so tact is involved—asking at the right time and in the right tone. You're not out to step on anyone's toes. I've found that many law enforcement officers are thrilled to be encouraged in their work. Almost all of them want to help people; it's why they got into the business. They appreciate putting a face with a name and being able to personalize the loss you've suffered. If you do encounter resistance at a lower level, go to the top. There's a police chief in every department, and no matter the department's size, investigating a fatality or a catastrophic injury is a big deal. It's perfectly appropriate to call the chief's secretary, introduce yourself, and say, as I did, "My mother was killed in your city on X date, and I'd like an opportunity to introduce myself to the chief and tell him or her a little bit about my family."

I recognize that we all come to the table with different experiences regarding the police and that many Blacks, among other American minorities, have come to fear the police as a hostile presence in their lives. But if you've suffered a catastrophic loss due to an accident, you have no choice but to count on the police. They are necessarily involved in what happens next, at least from a criminal law perspective. You can choose to do nothing to engage with them. Or you can choose to be empowered, to do what you can to have the highest level of participation in and influence over what unfolds.

YOUR THREE GOALS

You can regain some measure of control over the unthinkable by doing what you can to ensure that your loved one's case is more than just another file number to the police. By being proactive, you:

1. Put your family front and center by making it known that you're present and actively monitoring the investigation.

2. Personalize your loss and put a face to the name by sharing a photograph of your loved one.

3. Establish expectations for communication, timelines, and the role the police would like your family to play.

IF THE POLICE ASK TO SPEAK TO YOU

One final thought regarding the police: they may take the initiative and ask to speak to you or your family as part of their criminal investigation. If that happens, it's not because the family's in trouble. Instead, it's likely that they may be seeking information about the mental status, stability, or habits of your family member. They may ask you to come in and tell you they'll fill you in on what happened after they ask a few questions.

It's especially important for the family to feel empowered in those circumstances—to understand that they're under no obligation to comply. It may be something you want to do, as we've

just discussed, and I'm not suggesting there's necessarily something wrong with the police asking. But it's important to know
your rights.

First, it's voluntary. You don't have to do it. And if you want to
but don't feel comfortable in the moment, or aren't in the proper
state of mind, you can ask to delay.

You can also influence the terms under which you'll speak with
them. It is completely appropriate for you to ask the police to
explain their purpose and the subject matter to be discussed so
that you can decide whether you want to participate. They may
say they want to turn on a tape recorder; you can respond by
saying that first you want to know what they intend to ask you,
so you can determine whether you want it recorded or not. You
can also make your own recording of the conversation.

And of course, you can have your lawyer with you. Wanting to
have a lawyer help you navigate the situation doesn't suggest
that you've done anything wrong, and the police absolutely
understand that.

Again, I also believe there's value in talking with the police. It's a
two-way street. In our case, we wanted the Winter Park police to
know that transparent communication was extremely important
to us and were eager for as much information as we could get
from them without jeopardizing their investigation, even if the
information might be painful to hear. We also knew they were
likely to ask that the conversation be recorded, and we were fine
with that. But we began by telling them we had some things
to say about their communication and investigation that *they*
might not want recorded because the recordings would become
evidence in the event they brought charges. They agreed, and

we raised our concerns about how we had been treated to that point, three days after the accident—acknowledging that we knew they had our best interests in mind, but that we did not want to be left in the dark. I also told them that we'd had our own investigators on the ground, and I shared what we'd learned despite the silence from the police: that the concrete mixer truck driver came up from behind my mom as she was walking across the street with the right of way and the walk sign on and struck her while making a right-hand turn.

By the time we had finished, the police didn't want to record anything. The result was better communication with the police department going forward, and I believe the police were grateful that I hadn't expressed my displeasure about how our family had been treated in a recording that would become part of the public case file and potentially be used by a defense lawyer to call into question the quality of their investigation.

GETTING YOUR OWN EXPERTS ON THE GROUND

It could go without saying, but the police who investigate accidents get trained by someone. All police officers must be trained in accident reconstruction to at least a minimal degree in order to become certified. Once certified, an officer can work his or her way up through training at higher levels of accident reconstruction and investigation. With Level I training, an officer learns what to look for and what questions to ask at the scene but stops far short of learning how to reconstruct what happened. The highest certification is a Level IV reconstructionist, who is trained to use computer software to reconstruct and depict how a crash took place.

There are a multitude of experts *outside* police departments in an array of fields related to accident investigation, among them the instructors who train the police. These experts can be hired directly by a victim or surviving family members to conduct an independent private investigation. They may be most easily and economically located through a lawyer, as I'll explain, but they're accessible to anyone and can be located easily through a Google search.

Professional Engineers

Professional engineers are experts with academic education in a variety of specialties that, in many cases, goes far beyond the qualifications of people working within a police department. They might have both an undergraduate degree and a PhD in mechanical engineering. Others are known as human factors experts, with doctorates in assessing human decision-making: what someone might have seen, what their reaction time might have been, and other ways of understanding an accident from the human perspective. There are traffic engineers who spend their careers studying traffic light location and sequencing and the coordination of pedestrian walk signs and traffic lights. Others specialize in regulations related to commercial driver safety; still others might have a particular expertise in tractor-trailer safety or delivery trucks. There are independent experts who specialize in downloading and interpreting black box data in vehicles.

You can locate an accident reconstruction engineering firm by an online search for "Accident Reconstruction Engineer" along with the name of the city nearest to the crash. Call one of the firms and tell them that a loved one has been involved in a serious accident and that you are looking to consult with someone who can begin securing evidence from an independent perspective and work as a second set of eyes with the police department. As I discussed earlier in this chapter, evidence dissipates with every day that passes. Rather than paying for a full accident reconstruction from the onset, many times a good start is simply asking the firm what the estimated price would be to have them go to the crash location and secure the digital and physical evidence now that they will need to complete a full reconstruction should that prove necessary later.

Professional engineers work by the hour, and they're not cheap. A high-level professional engineer might require an upfront retainer of, say, $2,000 and may draw from it at the rate of $250 an hour or more. I'm aware of one who charges $200 an hour, less for his associate, with double time for rush, weekend, and night work.

The role of an engineer is analysis. As part of preserving evidence as I've described, they're likely to create a complete digital scan of the scene. That work will enable them to fully reconstruct the accident later if it proves necessary. You might spend $2,000 simply preserving the evidence you need to support a civil case.

Private Investigators

Less expensive than but equally important to hiring a forensic engineer is retaining a private investigator. Many will indicate on their websites if they work in accident investigation. The first and most important service you'll want them to provide is securing all video evidence from gas stations, residences, and other nearby cameras, as well as identifying and interviewing witnesses. They won't bring anything like the expertise of an engineer to the work; they can't conduct a digital scan, and they may overlook evidence that would catch an engineer's eye. But they may be able to go beyond what the police were able to do. The police don't look at systemic issues, such as a commercial driver's working conditions or how many other crashes the driver or company may have had in the past , because that is outside their role—but they can be highly relevant to understanding what's happened and holding the responsible party accountable. As I'll explain later, we found that to be the case. Private investigator rates typically range from $40 to $120 an hour, and you can get a lot done for $500.

Personal Injury Lawyers

I'm not here to make a sales pitch for personal injury lawyers, but an important option for the family is to work with a well-qualified law firm with a wealth of experience in catastrophic injury and wrongful death cases. I say "well-qualified" because, by simply reading this book, you may know more about handling these cases than many general practice lawyers or lawyers who specialize in other fields.

Lawyers who specialize in personal injury cases will begin with questions about who's at fault and whether there's insurance. If fault seems relatively clear and it appears there's insurance, most of these lawyers will take a case on what's called a contingency fee basis—a percentage of whatever settlement or award the family eventually wins.

That means the family doesn't need to come up with money to pay the lawyers by the hour—and a well-qualified personal injury law firm will front the cost for hiring the experts to secure the information necessary to reconstruct what happened. Lawyers also have relationships with engineers and private investigators whose work they trust and the ability to get them on the scene and working on the family's behalf as soon as possible. Typically, that is within twenty-four to forty-eight hours. If it's a credible firm and they later conclude there's no case to pursue, you won't be required to pay them back for the costs they've incurred.

ASSERTING CONTROL

The first phase in the aftermath of an accidental death or catastrophic injury is a police investigation. It may conclude at the scene within hours or unfold over the days and weeks that follow. If you take one thing away from reading this chapter, I hope it's this: you've been victimized by tragedy, and taking steps to protect yourself and your family from being re-victimized by the investigation represents an early and potentially very important means of asserting at least some control over the unthinkable.

CHAPTER 2

The Criminal Justice System

Following their two-month-long investigation, the Winter Park police decided to charge the concrete truck driver with careless driving resulting in death. If convicted, he would have faced the loss of his commercial driver's license for a year and a fine of one thousand dollars or more. Hardly in balance with the loss of my mother's life, but something.

When the police officer issued the ticket, she checked "careless driving" and forgot to check "resulting in death." A simple mistake; she literally forgot. The penalty: two points on his driver's license and a $180-fine. By the time the police recognized their error and issued the correct ticket, the driver had already pled guilty to the lower charge and had quickly paid the lower fine.

In court, the defense lawyer argued that because the driver had already pled guilty and paid the original ticket, he couldn't be charged a second time for the same event. I flew to Florida, not as a lawyer but as a victim, and begged the judge not to comply—but he did. The new charge was dismissed on the technicality. Which meant that, in the criminal justice system, the truck driver had gotten away with killing my mother and having it cost him less than if he were driving ten miles an hour over the speed limit—and he never lost his license to drive for a single day. I've met the police officer who wrote the ticket twice, and I like her. I'm sure she feels terrible about her mistake. But it's my family that has to live with the consequences, and it certainly left us feeling as if there wasn't much justice in the criminal justice system.

Unfortunately, we're not alone in that. Families who have endured a catastrophic loss are often extremely unhappy with the outcome of a criminal case—and it's not typically because of a mistake like failing to check a box. It's because of the system itself. The best way to explain why involves looking at who's involved in a criminal prosecution, how it works, and what it can and can't do for your family.

BRINGING CHARGES

Murder, robbery, assault, driving while intoxicated—these are all crimes under the law. Laws differ by state, but every written law spells out exactly what constitutes a crime as well as the penalties a wrongdoer could face.

Criminal charges can be brought in one of two ways. First, and most often, the police initiate a criminal case by arresting and charging someone with one or more crimes. The case is then handed off to a government prosecutor, who makes their own assessment and could choose to either drop the charges or pursue them.

Second, a prosecutor can bring charges independently, regardless of what the police did or didn't do. In the case of serious offenses, prosecutors will often begin by presenting evidence in private to a grand jury, whose decision serves as a preliminary indication of whether the community considers the case to be provable. After considering limited evidence presented by the prosecutor, a grand jury can return what's called an indictment as requested by the prosecutor.

That second mechanism is important to understand as a victim. It means that if the police don't press charges and you feel the family hasn't gotten a fair shake, you can go directly to the prosecutor's office and request an opportunity to talk with someone there about your case. Prosecutors are public employees, just like the police, and as a citizen, you certainly have a right to ask to speak with someone in their office. If the police decided not to bring charges, it's possible that the prosecutor's office won't even be aware of your case. In that event, you'll need to present them with documentation.

We've pursued just that course in my mother's case. Because of the mistake in issuing the ticket and the driver's quick plea and payment, the local prosecutor's office had not learned of her death and the circumstances surrounding it. We asked for an opportunity to meet and show them what was contained in the police file, in hopes they would consider an independent investigation into whether additional and more serious charges could be brought. The chief prosecutor agreed to meet with us. We used a PowerPoint presentation to make the case that the facts met the elements of vehicular homicide under Florida law. While sympathetic, the prosecutor expressed concern about proving the criminal intent required to convict the driver of that serious vehicular homicide charge. She expressed frustration with the Winter Park police department's failure to issue the right ticket and the lost opportunity to convict the driver of the lower level "careless driving resulting in death" charge. No new charges resulted, but in the end, we felt we had done all we could do in the criminal justice system on behalf of Big Sissy.

THE FACTORS PROSECUTORS CONSIDER

Before they pursue a criminal case involving catastrophic death or injury, regardless of who initiates the charges, prosecutors have to ask themselves a series of questions.

First is whether the person who'd be accused actually committed a crime as spelled out under the elements of the crime in the law. As I discussed in Chapter 1, the key issue impacting the seriousness of the charges filed in most death or catastrophic injury cases is criminal intent. A person who negligently caused an accident may be at fault for what happened without being guilty of a serious crime punishable with jail time. Someone who simply gets confused at an unfamiliar intersection, runs a red light, and causes a crash probably hasn't committed a serious crime. Someone who gets drunk, runs the same red light, and causes a crash has—because under the law, getting drunk and then driving is considered an expression of criminal intent.

The second question a prosecutor will ask themselves is whether they can prove the case without relying on testimony from the accused. The US Constitution protects all of us from being compelled to testify against ourselves—unless we willingly and knowingly confess. Without a confession, the prosecutor must rely on physical evidence and testimony from witnesses other than the accused person. Did cameras capture what happened? Do the people the police interviewed agree on what they saw?

Finally, the prosecutor must decide whether they can prove the case beyond a reasonable doubt. It's a very high standard, and that's intentional. It's not easy to win a criminal conviction. That's because our system was built, long ago, on the concept of individual rights and freedom. We decided, as a society, that we would rather see a guilty person go free than an innocent person be convicted.

THE PLAYERS AND THEIR ROLES

Let's say that criminal charges are brought in your family's case. How does it unfold from there? I'll begin by describing the primary participants and their roles.

Victim and Family

Most states have enacted victim's rights laws that establish meaningful support and opportunities for victims and their families, and I'll cover them in full in Chapter 3. That said, the victim (by which I mean the family too) is not formally involved in deciding whether to bring charges, what the charges should be, or whether to go to trial or negotiate a plea agreement with the accused. This stands in stark contrast to the civil justice system, where the victim makes all the decisions, beginning with whether to initiate a lawsuit in the first place which I will cover in Part 4.

The Prosecutor's Office

In some states, the chief prosecutors are called district attorneys, and in others, they're called state attorneys. In some instances, they're elected, and in others, they're appointed by the governor; either way, they serve a given term. At least one lawyer who works in the prosecutor's office will be assigned to every case; they're typically called an assistant state attorney or a deputy district attorney. The office will also employ its own investigators as well as victim rights advocates, who we'll cover in the next chapter. Crimes fall into different categories; the less serious are called "misdemeanors" and usually involve less than a year in jail or no jail time at all; the more serious crimes do and are called "felonies." Unfortunately, most catastrophic injury cases are charged as misdemeanors. Generally, the lesser the crime, the less experienced the prosecutor is likely to be.

If the case involves a ticket for careless or reckless driving, for example, you may be dealing with a prosecutor who's just out of law school, passed the bar exam a few months ago, and is filling an entry-level attorney position. If it's a DUI, the prosecutor's experience level may be a little higher. But generally speaking, unless you're talking about a serious intentional-act crime, such as first-degree murder, you'll likely be dealing with a prosecutor who has less than five years of experience. I'm not saying that's horrible; it's simply important to know who you're dealing with.

The Squeaky Wheel Effect

The prosecutor's office has a hierarchy, just as police departments do. There may be an elected official in charge—*the* state attorney or district attorney, with assistants who are the lawyers doing the work of the office. There may also be a career prosecutor within the structure, with a title such as bureau chief. As a family member, you can speak to the prosecutor assigned to your case and ask about their experience and the office hierarchy. If you're concerned about their experience, you can discuss it. It's not going to change their assignment, but it will achieve the same things I discussed in dealing with the police department: you'll put a name to the face, you'll let them know that you're watching and appreciative of their work, and you'll make sure they're aware that the family is engaged. It's the squeaky wheel effect again.

The Prosecutor's Role

The prosecutor in a case is responsible for all court appearances on behalf of the state, county, or city that brought the charges. They do not represent the victim; they represent the people. They're looking at the elements required to prove the case under the criminal laws asking themselves some of the same questions the police did: *Can I prove that? What witnesses do I need? Should we go to trial or negotiate a plea deal?* If the case does go to trial, it's the prosecutor who stands before the judge and jury to argue the case on behalf of the government.

For the Defense

If the person who is accused faces jail time, they have a right to a defense lawyer whether they can afford one or not. If they've got the money, they can hire a private lawyer who specializes in defending criminal cases. If they don't, they can have a public defender represent them. The public defender's office is funded by the government, but it serves to ensure that the rights of the accused are protected. Much of the criminal justice system is geared toward that objective, and for good reason: as a society, we value the rights of the individual and have a shared interest in ensuring that the government's profound policing powers are not abused.

The Defense Attorney's Role

As the counterpart to the prosecutor, the defense attorney makes appearances in court on behalf of the accused, enters their plea, represents them in any plea negotiations, and argues the case before the judge and jury if the case goes to trial. It's their job to file motions to suppress evidence or throw out charges in order to protect the interests of the accused. It can feel like a personal affront to you, as the victim's family, but it's their responsibility.

The Judge

Judges, depending on which state you are in, can either be elected or appointed to a given term in office. In almost all states, they're required to be lawyers. They can serve at either the state, county, or city level. Most cases, unless they involve felonies, are tried at the county level. Judges don't represent the victim, the people, or the accused. Their role is to ensure that the law is fairly applied, to make decisions on whether evidence meets the standards required to be considered, and to preside over the proceeding. They're the umpire, the referee, for the case.

So, it's the judge who sits up front as the charges against the accused are laid out in open court and who then schedules the case for trial. If there are disputes about the charges themselves or the evidence, the judge will schedule a hearing before deciding how to resolve them. Again, there are some people who believe the judge is there to help the victim and others who believe they're there to help the accused. They're not there to help either. Their job is to be even-handed in following the law.

The Jury

People accused of a crime in the United States have the right to request a trial by jury. They don't have to; they could request a trial by judge. But most people feel they'll have a better opportunity with a trial by jury. Perhaps they think jurors may mistrust the system; perhaps they think the judge will be hardened by all the cases he or she has heard; in any event, they'll choose a jury.

Typically, a jury in a criminal case consists of twelve people, though that is not always the case. They'll listen to the lawyers as they present the evidence and question witnesses, and when both sides are done the judge will instruct them on what has to be proven to convict someone of the crime or crimes involved. Each element of a given charge has to be proved beyond a reasonable doubt, which is a high standard; the judge will also instruct jurors to base their verdict on the evidence, not any sympathies or prejudices they may hold. If they believe the prosecutor has proven every element of a charge beyond a reasonable doubt, they are to deliver a verdict of guilty; if not, they are to render a verdict of not guilty. Finally, in a criminal case, the jury's verdict, as a group, must be unanimous.

THE MOST LIKELY OUTCOME

Regardless of the level of the charges being pursued, it is important for you to know that at the beginning the defense is very likely to enter a plea of not guilty. For the family, it can feel like a slap in the face to hear the accused enter that plea to something you know they did, but that's where the defense typically starts. They're trying to preserve their options, foremost of which is putting themselves in the best position to negotiate a plea bargain with the prosecutor. And the prosecutor is likely to listen. Their evidence may not be as strong as they'd like it to be; even if it is, anytime you go to trial there's always the chance you'll lose. What's more, the government's prosecution system is simply overwhelmed. If every criminal case that is filed were brought to trial, the system would collapse under the workload and defendants would go free because their cases weren't heard in a timely manner.

A plea bargain is just that. The accused agrees to plead guilty to a lesser offense than they've been charged with—an original charge, mind you, that the family often finds insufficient already. The accused might also agree to plead guilty to the original offense, with the prosecutor agreeing to recommend a lighter sentence. Even if they carelessly killed somebody, that can mean the accused will likely spend very little time, if any, in jail. Instead, they might pay what the court system considers a substantial fine—in the range of $1,000 or so—and agree to perform community service or submit to monitoring by a probation officer.

Depending on the circumstances and the history of the accused, some prosecutors may decide to stick with the original charges and not offer any plea bargain at all. If this is important to you and your family, then there are things you can do to actively participate as a crime victim in the criminal justice process that may help bring this about. (We will cover that in Chapter 3.) But more times than not, what we see happen is that the prosecutor will offer some incentive for the at-fault person to enter a plea rather than taking the criminal case to trial. That incentive may be pleading guilty to a lesser charge, or it may mean offering to propose that the judge enter a lighter sentence for a guilty plea to the original charge.

Such an outcome is rarely satisfying to the family. But it is the most likely outcome of a criminal case, just the same.

THE TIMEFRAME

What most often takes the longest in a criminal case involving a fatality or catastrophic injury is the police or prosecutor's investigation itself: that is, the time from when the event occurs until there's a decision made to proceed with criminal charges. If we're talking about an accident only involving property damage, the police are going to come to the scene and do an investigation, then issue a ticket in the next twenty-four hours, if not right then and there. In an accident involving a fatality, it can take months.

Once charges are formally filed in the criminal justice system, the accused has the right to a speedy trial under the US Constitution. The Constitution doesn't define specifically what that means, so it varies some from state to state. Let's say it's 180 days; that would be typical. If the prosecutor doesn't meet that timeline, the accused can demand that the criminal charges be dropped.

One reason months can pass before a criminal case is initiated is because the prosecutor wants to be sure they have their ducks in a row before filing charges in case they are rushed to trial. But in most cases, after formal charges are actually filed, the defense waives the right to a speedy trial as a tactic. That slows the process, putting the case in a much slower docket, or list of cases. It can take up to a year before such a case is actually heard in court.

We most often see a timeframe ranging from four months to a year between the bringing of criminal charges to final resolution. That doesn't include any jail time the accused may face or an appeal. The wheels of justice in America turn—but they don't necessarily turn quickly.

THE STEPS IN A CRIMINAL CASE

We've covered most of these already, but I thought it would be helpful to lay out the steps in a criminal case in one place.

1. An arrest is made or a ticket is issued (or not).

2. The prosecutor decides to proceed with the case (or not).

3. The accused makes their first appearance in court for a formal reading of charges and enters a plea. This is also called an "arraignment"; the defense often waives the appearance. If they don't, it may be the family's first chance to see the person who killed or injured their loved one.

4. The accused asks to remain out of jail or to be released pending trial (or not). The judge may set bail, a sum the accused must provide as a guarantee they will appear for trial, or may allow the accused to remain free pending trial with no bail requirement at all.

5. The judge sets a trial date.

6. The discovery period begins. Here the prosecution is required to reveal all of its evidence to the accused, so the defense can prepare.

7. The plea negotiations take place (or not). As we've already discussed, most cases end not in a trial but a plea agreement.

8. The case is tried (or not).

9. The jury reaches a verdict.

10. If the verdict is guilty or a plea agreement is reached, the judge sets a date for sentencing. Here, the victim—by which I also mean the family—has a right to make a statement. So does the accused.

11. The accused goes to jail, pays a fine, performs community service, or is assigned to the probation department to ensure that terms of the sentence are met.

REALITIES OF RESTITUTION

When a person pleads guilty or is found guilty of a crime, the judge may order the payment of restitution as part of the punishment. Restitution requires a person convicted of a crime to compensate the victim for the actual financial losses they sustained. In doing so, the judge will only consider financial losses or expenses that were directly caused by the crime. And you have to provide documentation of the loss to have it considered. You can request restitution for things like funeral, medical, and mental health expenses. Lost wages, travel, and any other expense incurred by the victim and immediate family members can also be considered if documentation is submitted.

In general, restitution is another facet of the criminal justice system that can sometimes leave families frustrated. A criminal court will not require the guilty person to compensate, through restitution, for what are called non-economic losses: the formal name for your grief, pain and suffering, loss of enjoyment of life, mental anguish, and other emotional harms. The civil justice system can. (We will cover the civil justice system in Part 4.)

As a practical matter, most criminal courts will only require payment of restitution for out of pocket expenses that are not already covered by insurance. It's not always entirely black and white. I have seen a judge order the payment of restitution for funeral and burial expenses, even though they could also be recovered through a burial or funeral insurance policy. An immediate family member who flies into town for the funeral may have a restitution claim to recover their travel expenses. The same is true for wages lost while at the hospital, providing support to an injured family member, or while at home, grieving a death and unable to work. And restitution does usually cover insurance deductibles and copayments. But as a general rule, if an expense is covered by insurance, it's unlikely you will recover it through restitution.

Why? The criminal justice system does not want to serve as a long term collection agency. It doesn't want to permit double recovery either: getting the same compensation from *both* the criminal system and from insurance companies. And it does not want to create conditions in a sentence that the accused couldn't possibly fulfill. Consider a case of careless driving resulting in death, for example. If the accused was ordered to pay restitution of $500,000, but they didn't have assets sufficient to cover it, they'd be in violation of their criminal sentence and unable to ever get out from under the criminal justice system.

So, typically what you'll see is restitution on the order of $5,000 to $15,000—much smaller amounts than the family would consider fair punishment. Generally, it's the district attorney or prosecutor who is responsible for providing the judge with the amount of restitution owed to the crime victim based on documentation the victim provides. Make sure you talk to the prosecutor's office about the documentation needed to support your claim for restitution.

REALITIES OF PROSECUTION

Most prosecutors are working that job because they care tremendously about people and want to play a critical role in keeping our communities safe. But the practical reality is also that these are government-run offices that are underfunded, overworked, and understaffed. That means the people in charge of the office have no choice but to prioritize the cases they handle. One factor is societal concerns; at present, domestic violence cases are highly prioritized. Human nature also plays a role. Anyone who invests their time and effort in trial work has an interest in winning. So, prioritizing involves picking winners too.

What's most likely to be plea-bargained? Crimes that are lower priorities and cases with weaker evidence. Another factor favoring plea bargains: cases in which the accused has no prior convictions.

REALITIES OF SENTENCING

The realities of sentencing are similar to the realities of prosecution: we can't keep everybody in jail, in part because our prisons are already overcrowded and in part because it wouldn't be good for society. As a result, political decisions must be made as to who we're going to put in jail and why.

At the time formal charges are initiated, unless a case involves an intentional act—driving under the influence (DUI), drug use, or fleeing the scene of an accident—the person accused of causing catastrophic injury or death is generally released immediately on bail or their own recognizance, meaning they either post some money or give their word that they'll appear for trial. So, they don't spend any time in jail pre-trial.

Once someone is convicted, the government's interest may still be in alternatives to jail time because of the reasons I've described. For misdemeanors—again, this means most cases—with full conviction and empty prisons, the accused would still spend just a year or less behind bars, most often in a county jail, a less restrictive setting than a state prison.

Let's say someone is jailed with a sentence of six months. They may be out in as little as three months in some jurisdictions because of good behavior; after all, the government has an interest in rewarding inmates for not causing problems while they're there.

Put it all together, and you'll find that—unless we're talking about intentional harm or DUI—in most cases involving death or catastrophic injury, there's very little jail time ever served. That's particularly true for first offenders.

WHERE THIS LEAVES FAMILIES

Typically, the criminal justice process leaves families facing the consequences of a catastrophic injury or death feeling very frustrated and disappointed. The exception is most often cases involving DUIs. If we're talking about someone with three previous DUIs who kills another person in a fourth DUI event, bringing that case to trial is going to be a very high priority for the prosecutor's office. They'll put their most highly skilled, hard-nosed lawyer on the case and try to put the accused in prison for as long as the law permits. But, again, that is the exception. In cases of death and traumatic injury, most families looking at the scales of justice at the end of the criminal case see the tremendous losses that they have suffered on one side of the scales and the minimal consequences and punishment suffered by the person who caused all of it on the other side of the scale. And the scales are nowhere close to balancing—which, after all, is the basic metaphor for justice: the lady justice, blindfolded and holding a scale that's in balance.

As a general rule, families want the highest measure of justice the system can provide and a speedy resolution. But it's not TV; cases often last a year, not an hour. Families may consider the initial charge to fall short of the loss they've suffered. They may see evidence excluded from the trial. No matter how good the reasons may be for a plea bargain, they may find the outcome offensive because of how it dilutes the nature of the offense itself.

I share all of this in hopes of preparing you for what to expect, not to condemn the system. Remember, in the criminal justice system the standard for winning a conviction is a high bar—and it's intended to be. The system is built on a belief that we would rather see a guilty person go free than an innocent person be convicted.

The good news is that there are other avenues available to victims that go beyond the criminal justice system and that can help victims get answers, retribution, and justice. (I will cover those in Part 4.) In addition, there are proactive steps we will discuss in Chapter 3 that you can take within the criminal justice system that will give your family a measure of control in that process. These steps will help to ensure your family has a seat at the table when important decisions are being made and that you are heard loud and clear by the prosecutor, the judge, and the person who caused all the harm in the first place.

My law firm recently worked with a family who had lost a loved one in an accident caused by an older driver who had only $150,000 worth of insurance and no recoverable assets beyond that. We did not wait on the prosecutor to proceed as they saw fit. Instead, we told the at fault driver and her lawyer directly that we would only consider accepting the limited insurance money to settle a potential civil case if the driver agreed to enter a straight-up guilty plea to the original charge of careless driving resulting in death and not ask for any leniency in the criminal case, instead accepting whatever sentence the judge handed down. We also insisted that the driver agree to read a letter from the victim's family that told the story of their lost loved one and the impact the death had on the family left behind. The family wanted the at-fault driver to stand up in the courtroom, admit fault, and accept full responsibility for what she had done. The victim's family, which was very religious, told the driver they wanted to forgive her—but that had to begin with her accepting responsibility. The driver agreed and replied with a letter to the family so heartfelt that it made me cry when I read it.

By asserting themselves, the family in this case achieved a result that will carry everyone involved a long way toward healing.

Even if your circumstances don't permit that or it's not a path you choose, you do have rights—and support—within the criminal justice process. For that we have victim's rights laws to thank, and we'll take them up next.

CHAPTER 3

Victim's Rights

In recent decades, victim's rights laws have been enacted in almost every state, and in many cases, they're now embedded in state constitutions, which gives them even greater weight. It's meaningful progress toward finding a balance between the rights of the accused and those who've been victimized—and it's largely the result of advocacy by victims themselves. Most notable among them are President Ronald Reagan, who survived an assassination attempt in 1981, and the family of Marsalee Nicholas, a college student killed by an ex-boyfriend in 1983.

As president, Ronald Reagan was arguably the most powerful political figure in the world at the time he was shot—and yet in the criminal justice system, he found he had no voice. In proclaiming the first-ever National Crime Victims' Week, Reagan said, "We need a renewed emphasis on, and an enhanced sensitivity to, the rights of victims. These rights should be a central concern of those who participate in the criminal justice system, and it is time all of us paid greater heed." He also created a national task force that concluded the system was imbalanced in favor of the accused and at the expense of victims.

Many families picked up the cause, and the breakthrough came with Marsy's Law, enacted in a referendum in California in

2008. It established seventeen specific rights for victims under California law, and the campaign to pass it evolved into the Marsy's Law nonprofit, which is dedicated to the enactment and enforcement of victim's rights laws across the country. As a result of this advocacy, millions of people in the United States who have lost loved ones to death or who have suffered catastrophic injury now have specific protections in the criminal justice system that they didn't have before.

Among the states that have enacted victim's rights laws is Florida, where my mother was killed. That law enabled us to file what's called an "appearance"with the court that said, in essence, "Hey, we're here, we're the victims, and we want to avail ourselves of our constitutional rights in this case, beginning with being notified of all proceedings." Without these notifications, we would have had to go online and repeatedly check the court website to obtain basic information about the criminal case, including the next court proceeding, when the driver would next have to appear in court, when the arraignment might take place, when the trial might begin, and so on. But once you have entered an appearance in the case, you get notification of each step in the unfolding process at the same time the accused and their lawyer do. That is just the beginning of what victim's rights laws provide for.

WHAT'S THE LAW IN YOUR STATE?

For a list of states with victim's rights laws as of 2021, as well as information on how to find the details of the rights they establish, turn to Appendix 1. (You can find the same list with clickable links to the actual laws on my website, *KyleBachus.com*.)

WHO'S A VICTIM?

The first question a victim's rights law addresses is who actually qualifies as a "victim." This definition is consistent across most states—and you may be surprised to learn who is and who isn't included in the definition.

First of all, of course, the person against whom an act is committed is the victim; if they are a minor, then their parents or legal guardians are considered victims too.

If the victim has died, then their immediate family members are considered victims under the law. Having been divorced since I was a kid, my mom wasn't married when she died, but my dad is still alive. She had two living sisters and three living children with a total of seven grandchildren.

Only my brother, sister, and I—her children—legally qualified as immediate family members.

If a catastrophic injury leaves the victim mentally incapacitated, then the person they've designated or who has been appointed to act on their behalf would also be considered a victim under the law. Beyond that representative, though, even immediate family members may not be included.

Despite these restrictions, my advice is that if you feel like you're a victim, go ahead and file an appearance with the criminal court. Put yourself in a position to be afforded the rights under your state's law until somebody says, "I'm sorry, but you don't qualify." And by all means, read the law in your state to see if you qualify; understanding what the law provides for can be empowering in and of itself. Generally speaking, though, the victim's rights laws cover the victim themselves, their designee or legal guardian, or their surviving immediate family members.

In reading your state's law, you'll often find a list of the crimes that it covers. It will certainly include felonies, the most serious crimes punishable by more than a year in jail, and misdemeanors, the lesser crimes punishable with a year in jail or less. And in most cases, it will specifically cover careless or reckless driving that results in serious bodily injury or death, such as the circumstances in which my mother died.

THE GOALS AND LIMITS OF VICTIM'S RIGHTS

Generally speaking, victim's rights laws have four primary, practical goals. They are intended to make sure that crime victims have the opportunity to be:

- Informed
- Present
- Heard
- Supported

These rights apply through the entire criminal justice process, from the moment the crime investigation begins through the trial to the parole and probation process intended to guide the life of the person responsible for your loss.

The limits of victim's rights laws are important to understand too. They do *not* give victims decision-making power within the criminal justice system. So, you'll have no formal control over how a case is investigated, whether or not to file charges, what charges to file, whether to negotiate a plea agreement, how a case is tried, or what sentence is imposed. The decisions are for others to make.

These limitations don't sound very good, I know. But victim's rights laws do guarantee you a place at the table if you want to express yourself and provide input as a crime victim to the police and prosecutors who have control; as I've discussed in Chapters 1 and 2, that matters. Generally speaking, I believe that everybody involved in the criminal justice system is there because they want to help people and do justice, from the police officer to the prosecutor and the judge. If we give everybody the benefit of the doubt, as we should, then your active involvement in the process has incredible potential to actually influence the outcome and that is exactly what we have seen happen with many of the victims that my law firm has been privileged to represent. If you're there and present, it can impact the decisions that others make—and it will give you considerable insight into why decisions are made and a better understanding of the process.

Victim's rights laws can also provide tangible support in two forms that we'll cover: a victim's advocate to help you understand and navigate the criminal justice process as well as victim's compensation funds that can provide significant financial assistance.

UNDERSTANDING YOUR RIGHTS

After they've made their initial contact with the family following a traumatic death, under most victim's rights laws, the police are required to provide the victim with a written copy of their rights. This means that when the police arrive in their cruiser bearing bad news, they should give you both a card with their contact information—it's just like a business card—and a pamphlet that outlines your rights under the law.

In most states, the pamphlet should inform you not only of your rights but also how to go about acting on them. It contains information on the services and resources available to you, including accessing the police report at no charge, the availability of victim's compensation benefits, or getting a protective order if your circumstances warrant it. The pamphlet should also inform you of the timeframe within which the police are required to return any property they have taken in the course of their investigation.

DIDN'T GET THE PAMPHLET?

If the officer left you with a business card but not the pamphlet, just reach out to the investigating officer and ask for a copy: "Could you provide me with a written copy of my rights and resources as a crime victim in our state?"

VICTIM'S RIGHTS AND THE PROSECUTOR

As I've discussed, victim's rights laws don't give you control over decisions the prosecutor makes. But in most states, thanks to victim's rights laws, the victim is entitled to be kept informed of the decisions prosecutors make at every critical stage in the process. Maybe even more important, victims are also guaranteed the opportunity to express their wishes as the case unfolds.

The list of steps you'll be notified of in most states is extensive and includes:

- When (or if) a case is opened; what the charges are going to be
- The name, address, and telephone number of the lawyer responsible for prosecuting the case
- The internal case file number
- The courtroom to which the case is assigned
- Whether a warrant has been issued for an arrest
- If the prosecutor determines that charges originally brought by the police are unfounded, or chooses to reduce or decide to pursue some but not all of them
- Whether and when the accused will be released from jail or get their bail reduced
- The opportunity to provide a written victim's impact statement to the prosecutor detailing how your loss has affected the family, which will likely be shared with the judge, the defendant, and their lawyer
- The time and place of every critical stage in the process and whether you have a right to be present and heard
- The opportunity to speak with the prosecutor before a case is plea-bargained and the right to be informed of the terms
- In some states, the opportunity to a copy of the pre-sentence report, which details, among other things, the defendant's prior record
- The opportunity to consult with the prosecutor following a conviction about what the family wishes the sentence to be, within the range allowed by the law

- When and where sentencing is going to occur and your right to be heard before the sentence is issued
- The opportunity to request a hearing on the appropriate amount of restitution, given the limitations discussed in Chapter 2

Most prosecutors are anxious to hear what victims want; they sympathize with and want to help you achieve justice. But if the prosecutor's office doesn't reach out to you, you are empowered to take the initiative by calling to request a meeting. You are also entitled to know the hierarchy of the office and ask to speak to someone higher up.

It's a good idea to be proactive. The practice in our firm is to send a formal letter to the prosecutor's office in every catastrophic injury or death case that we handle, clearly documenting the family's desire to have the prosecutor's office adhere to their obligations under the victim's rights law. I'd recommend you send such a letter yourself or ask your lawyer to do so.

SAMPLE: LETTER TO THE PROSECUTOR'S OFFICE

You'll find a sample letter to the prosecutor's office in Appendix 2.

If you decide to attend the criminal proceedings, victim's rights laws typically require the prosecutor to advise you of your right to be transported to and from the court and to financial assistance for missing work. They should also provide referrals to childcare, elder care, or disabled care assistance if you need it to ensure that you are available to testify. If your employer gives you difficulty about missing work to testify, the prosecutor is empowered to reach out on your behalf to ensure that you face no consequences for doing so.

VICTIM'S RIGHTS AND THE JUDGE

As the victim, your involvement with the judge is far more limited than with the police and prosecutors. Again, the judge's role is to ensure that the case proceeds in a fair and constitutional manner and, ultimately, to determine restitution and sentence the defendant if convicted. They are the referee. But as a victim, you do have a right to address the court during the sentencing phase of the criminal case—to speak in open court or to read a letter to the court explaining how the crime has impacted your family and to tell the court the family's feelings regarding an appropriate sentence or punishment. Most judges want to hear from the victims as part of their decision-making process. You may ultimately disagree with the judge's decision, but if you exercise this right, you will have been heard, and you will have done everything in your control to obtain the best result for your family in the criminal justice system.

Being Present

It is important to make sure that the judge, through the court filing, is aware that you're a victim and that you're engaged in the process and want to be kept informed. This is somewhat duplicative, of course, because the prosecutor is supposed to perform

that function. But what if they don't? This is where filing the
entry of appearance document that I discussed in the opening of
the chapter comes into play. These can be submitted by mail or,
these days, electronically. It's not that hard. You'll need the case
number and will simply state that you're the victim in the case
and would like to be advised of all the proceedings. If there's a
victim's rights law in your state, you can make reference to it or
simply attach a copy; if nothing else, it will show that you know
what you're doing.

> ### SAMPLE: ENTRY OF APPEARANCE
>
> You'll find a sample entry of appearance in Appendix 3.

Entering an appearance will ensure that you receive the same
notices at the same time everyone else involved in the case does.
It's not a question of access; we have open, public courthouses
and open, public trials. It's a question of knowing when to be
there and what's at issue.

Being Heard

In almost all states, at certain critical stages the judge is required
to ask if the victim is present and wishes to be heard. Again, it's
best to be proactive. If you attend criminal court proceedings,
you can approach the clerk in the courtroom and notify them
that you're present. They will inform the judge. When the case
is called, you can stand up, and the judge will probably then ask
who you are there on behalf of and if you have anything to say
regarding the matter at hand.

Behaving with Respect

It's very important to be respectful, no matter how much you like or dislike what's happening. That may not be easy. It can be a very emotional experience to walk into a courtroom, where you may find yourself face-to-face with the person responsible for your loss. They may show remorse—and they may not. You might dislike what their lawyer has to say when defending their client; it can be very hurtful. But the judge is going to demand appropriate conduct from everyone in the courtroom, and there will be police officers present to enforce order. Nobody should speak out of turn. Anybody in a courtroom—including the victim—can be held in contempt of court for failing to listen to a judge's instruction. The bottom line is that, as the victim, you are entitled to play a role in the criminal justice process. You don't want to jeopardize these hard-won rights for future victims—and there is nothing that prevents a judge from ordering that you're kept out of future proceedings based on inappropriate or disruptive behavior.

VICTIM'S RIGHTS AFTER CONVICTION

As we've discussed, most cases involving traumatic death and catastrophic injury are misdemeanors, with jail time of no more than a year. Cases involving habitual offenders or DUIs may be felonies with stiffer penalties. In any case, once a person is sentenced, victim's rights laws in most states entitle you to be notified of actions taken by the corrections department. But in many states, there's an important difference at this stage of the process: as a victim, you're required to make a request in writing in order to take advantage of this right.

The court system's notification process should tell you where the person is being incarcerated, and you'll need to send your request there. By doing that, you establish a right to be notified if the person is transferred, released, or escapes. This includes being notified in advance of any transfer to a non-secure half-way house as they transition back into the community. You also have a right to be notified of any parole hearings, which may result in an early release from prison. In many states, you have a right to submit a victim's statement to the parole board regarding your wishes, and you have the right to be notified of the board's decision.

It's also possible that the person responsible for your loss may be put on probation, either without serving any jail time or following their release. This requires them to submit to monitoring by probation officers to ensure that they comply with the terms of their sentence; if they don't, probation can be revoked, and they'll go to jail. Once again, the court system is obligated to tell you the location and phone number of the probation department, and you can make a similar request to be informed of developments in the case to the probation agency. Once you've submitted that request, you have a right to be informed of any hearing regarding a change or early termination of probation, to be heard before a decision is made, and to be notified of the outcome. You also have the right to be notified if there's a transfer in jurisdiction for any reason—and you'll even be notified if they fail to complete the terms of their probation because they've died.

SAMPLE: LETTER TO CORRECTIONS AND PROBATION

You'll find a sample letter to a corrections agency or probation department in Appendix 4.

IF THE DEFENDANT IS A JUVENILE

Let's say the person responsible for your loss was a juvenile under the law, which would typically mean they're under the age of eighteen. Most such cases are handled confidentially within the juvenile justice system, where significant privacy rights are provided for the juveniles involved. Access to information is much more limited than in cases where the offender is an adult. But victim's rights laws generally don't place limitations on the rights they grant because the accused is a juvenile. My advice is to move forward in exercising your rights just as you would if an adult were involved and see what you run up against.

VICTIM'S ADVOCATES

Because of victim's rights laws, it's common now to find victim's advocates employed within the police department or prosecutor's office. These are special people. They're not there because the pay is high; it's typically not. They're there because they have an affinity for helping victims. Many have been victims of crimes themselves or have had family members who were victims. This has become their calling.

Their job is to help victims understand the process and to support them as the process unfolds. They're not involved in investigating or prosecuting the case; they're there for you. They may walk you through your state's victim's rights law. If you're entering an appearance to ensure you're kept informed, they may agree to review it for you. They may make referrals to services you need. If you're scared by the thought of going to court, they may accompany you. They may even be the first person you hear from after the police officer notifies you of your loss.

Lean on these advocates. They are on your side!

STATE CRIME VICTIMS COMPENSATION PROGRAMS

Let's say you're a breadwinner and are supposed to go to work the next day or the day after—but you can't because something terrible has just happened to your family. Perhaps your employer will give you time off, but it's unpaid.

Almost every state provides victims of crime with access to what is called a Victim's Compensation Fund. These funds are intended to provide prompt financial assistance to crime victims and cover a broad range of expenses, including:

- Lost wages
- Child care
- Airfare and hotel expenses
- Rental car expenses
- Funeral expenses
- Grief counseling services

These are government benefits. They're funded every time someone pays a speeding or traffic ticket or criminal fine as part of sentencing. A portion of the fine that's collected goes to the Victim's Compensation Fund. The crime victim's rights pamphlet that is available through the police department or prosecutor's office isn't likely to detail these benefits, but it should give you contact information and possibly a website enabling you to contact your state's Victim's Compensation Fund program for information on how to apply for these benefits.

In some cases, assistance is immediately available. One of the really helpful things about these benefits is that access to financial assistance is not dependent on a conviction in the criminal case, which, as we've discussed, might not come until a year down the road. To trigger the benefits, the police simply have to believe there is probable cause that a crime has been committed, and you have to fall under the state's definition of a crime victim.

There will be an application process, and it can take from a couple of weeks to a month or more before you actually get the money. But the people who run the program in your state can walk you through the application process and put you in touch with the support services you need immediately. The victim's advocate you're assigned will be able to help you access these benefits. Many funeral homes won't charge the family anything so long as there is an application for victim's compensation benefits pending that seeks payment of the funeral expenses.

The laws in many states provide a total reimbursement cap for all the expenses they cover. In Colorado, it's currently $30,000.

BE PROACTIVE

The spread of victim's rights laws is a story of hope, written through the advocacy of others who endured losses such as yours. As we've discussed, they don't put you in the position of controlling the criminal justice process—but they do ensure you'll be heard if you choose to be and that you'll have access to important benefits and support if you need them. You're not required to take advantage of any of these rights; it's your choice.

One problem with victim's rights laws is that they don't have an enforcement mechanism if the rights they establish aren't respected. You can fall through the cracks, and there's no re-do of the process if you miss an opportunity to be heard or supported as a result.

That is why taking the initiative matters. You have to know your rights, and you have to take action in order to exercise them. I hope this chapter has helped you understand why and what benefits you'll see if you do.

We've now covered the criminal justice side of a traumatic death or catastrophic injury, from the role of the police to the workings of a criminal case as it unfolds and the rights you have as a victim. But there's much more to the turmoil you'll face in the aftermath of your loss—and it comes at you fast, from all directions. I think of these as collateral, everyday issues, and we'll take them up next.

> If you've experienced the sudden death of a loved one, Parts 2 and 4 are most relevant to you. You can decide to skip Part 3. If your loved one has suffered a catastrophic injury, you can decide to skip Part 2 and go directly to Parts 3 and 4.

PART II

Practical Challenges for Families after a Traumatic Death

The cats: April and Addie. My mother treasured them as companions. And on the night of her death, they were alone in her home, hungry for dinner, wondering where she'd gone, waiting for her to return.

Of the dozens of practical and sometimes difficult challenges that bombard you in the aftermath of a loved one's catastrophic death, caring for their pets is one of the most immediate. My sister drove down to my mother's house the next morning to take care of April and Addie's immediate needs, but neither she, my brother, nor I could bring them permanently into our home.

We knew how important it would have been to my mom to keep them together, but that's a big ask for anyone. What to do?

We started with Facebook. Less than forty-eight hours after Mom was killed, my wife shared a picture of the cats and our dilemma on my mom's Facebook account, and my mom's sister did the same with a neighbor's Facebook account, all in hopes of finding the cats a new home. One of those who saw the post thought of her parents: professors who were retiring from Stetson University in Florida and talking about getting a cat. They were willing. We took April and Addie to a veterinarian to make sure they'd had their shots and were in good health, and the professors drove an hour and a half, each way, to bring them to their new home. They still text us occasionally with photographs.

We couldn't have found a better resolution to that challenge—but as I've said, it was just one of dozens of practical issues that we faced following my mother's death, and many of them were upon us immediately. We were stunned. It felt overwhelming; I expect that's a feeling you recognize.

Knowledge is power, and it's critical to regaining some sense of control.

In this section of the book, I'll walk through some of the challenges you may face in hopes of making them more manageable. We'll begin with chapters dedicated to the issues surrounding a loved one's traumatic death, some of which will apply in cases of catastrophic injury too, and then I'll take up the issues specific to catastrophic injury alone.

CHAPTER 4

The Remains

This is a tough topic, and if much time has passed since your loved one's death, it may no longer be relevant—but we need to talk about the body.

If the person who died was killed instantly and therefore didn't get transported for medical care, then their body is typically taken directly to the medical examiner's office. If they died in the hospital, their body typically goes to the medical examiner's office next.

ABOUT THE MEDICAL EXAMINER

The medical examiner is a public official responsible for identifying the cause of death. They're generally appointed and are always physicians, usually specialists in forensic pathology. Medical examiners perform autopsies, examine injuries and collect and analyze blood and tissue samples.

Depending on the circumstances, the medical examiner's office may ask you to identify your loved one's remains. For some families, it's an important step toward closure—completing the story of their loved one, in some sense, and making their death real. (And of course, the opportunity to identify the body may come at the funeral home or the crematorium too.)

In our case, the accident that killed my mother rendered her unrecognizable. I don't know that I would have had the courage to go see my mom, but my brother, a doctor, certainly would have. Without that opportunity, it's as if we are missing something important in the story of her life.

We were asked to identify my mom by photographs the medical examiner's office took of her cell phone, her driver's license, and the bloodstained jewelry she was wearing. We recognized them all. Then, we were asked to sign an affidavit—a sworn statement—identifying her based on the circumstantial evidence we had seen.

Autopsies

If the cause of death is not immediately clear, the medical examiner may do an autopsy to determine the cause of death. It does not happen in every case. If the medical examiner considers it necessary, there's no cost to the family; it's a public expense, paid by taxpayers.

There may be instances where the medical examiner doesn't consider an autopsy necessary, but the family wants one done. You're entitled to ask, but you need to do so promptly. Autopsies are best if performed within twenty-four hours of death and ideally before embalming, which can obviously interfere with blood tests. But autopsies performed later and even on exhumed bodies may still provide vital information, depending on the circumstances.

I once handled a case in which a thirty-year-old man suffered a severe broken leg in a crash. He underwent surgery in a hospital and died from a blood clot on his third day there. The family cremated the body, assuming an autopsy had been done. It hadn't been. They were left to ask, "What happened? We said good night to him one night, and the next day, he's dead?"

Instances such as this don't come up very often. But if there's any question in your mind about what caused your loved one's death, you can request that an autopsy be performed even if the medical examiner doesn't consider it necessary. The cost for a private autopsy is not covered by Medicare, Medicaid, or private health insurance, but some hospitals will cover the cost for an autopsy if requested by the family for a patient who died in their hospital. Otherwise, you likely will have to pay out of pocket for a private autopsy.

If for some reason the local medical examiner's office doesn't have the capacity, you can call other medical examiner's offices in your area and ask whether they would be available to do a private autopsy. The National Association of Medical Examiners (www.thename.org) maintains a list of resources to help find private autopsy providers. You can also locate a board-certified forensic pathologist by doing a Google search for "Private Autopsy" and adding the name of your city to the search. Be sure to ask in advance what the cost would be. The current average cost for a private autopsy is between $2,000 and $3,000.

Autopsies usually take about two to four hours to perform, but the full results may take four to six weeks to prepare.

Here's something else important to remember: once a body is cremated, you lose out on the opportunity for an autopsy.

Keepsakes

Here's one more thing with long-term consequences that can be achieved only while the body remains available: keepsakes. These can be meaningful to loved ones for years to come. The funeral home or crematorium may raise the topic, but if they don't, you may not even think to ask. And there are things that can be done.

I can tell you that preserving a keepsake helped my family. We had my mother's fingerprint taken before her cremation, and we made the image available to family members on pendants. We ended up getting four or five. Nobody was asked to wear them, or expected to, but they were a keepsake.

My sons asked for one, and I don't think they are ready yet to look at it. But they can. It's there whenever they need it.

My daughter, who is a little older, wears hers every day, in a pendant dangling around her neck. It's that important to her.

What's important for you to know is that preserving a keepsake such as this is possible—and that the opportunity to do so lasts only as long as the body is present and available. In some states, the Victim's Compensation Fund (see Chapter 3) will even cover the cost.

PAYING FOR THE FUNERAL

Once your loved one's body is transferred to a funeral home, one of the next issues you'll face is who's going to pay for it. Funeral homes don't work for free, and the decision needs to be made quickly.

First off, it's important to know that these are ultimately expenses of the estate. That means if there's money in the estate, it can be used to reimburse the person who paid for funeral expenses.

And as we discussed in Chapter 3, Victim's Compensation Funds also cover funeral expenses. In most cases, the funeral home will be aware of these funds and are willing to assist you in accessing that money. So can the victim's advocate who is working with you.

Here's a benefit your family may not know about: if your loved one ever served in the US military, the military will pay for the funeral and burial or cremation. You can pick one of 142 military cemeteries around the country, and the military will pay for both the funeral and burial there.

It's also possible that your loved one bought insurance to cover their funeral expenses. I recalled my mother saying something about doing just that, and as we went through her papers, we came across it, in the form of a $5,000-life insurance policy. My mother had listed all three of her children as beneficiaries. We had already taken care of her funeral costs by then, but we simply filed a claim and provided a copy of her death certificate to receive the money, which came in the portions due each of us in three checks. You may find that the person listed as the beneficiary of a funeral policy isn't the one who actually paid for the funeral; in that case, you'll have to work it out. Whether the beneficiary chooses to do the right thing with the money is their decision and no one else's.

ARRANGING A MILITARY FUNERAL

The National Cemetery Administration, part of the US Department of Veterans Affairs, is responsible for handling these burials. You can find the information you'll need on its website: www.cem.va.gov/burial_benefits/index.asp.

Entering "national cemetery burial information" in a Google search will bring you there too. You could also ask your victim's advocate for help.

One thing to note: you'll have to provide proof of your loved one's military service.

Finally, if your loved one's death involved a car accident, many car insurance policies also provide a funeral benefit that may apply whether they were in their own car or not. That means even if they were walking or riding a bike and were hit by a car, their funeral expenses could be covered, typically up to a limit of $5,000 or $10,000.

If all else fails, most funeral homes will offer credit. You could pay with a credit card or arrange to make payments.

CHAPTER 5

Their Online Life

My mother was our family's unofficial photographic historian. By the time she died, she had created or was working on as many as 500 Shutterfly books that documented our lives together over the years. Some she had printed out and shared, but many existed only on the Shutterfly platform. They are a cherished dimension of her role in our family's life. And if we had not been able to access her account, all of that work would have been lost to us.

That is just one example of a modern challenge: the importance of getting access to your loved one's online life—and particularly their social media accounts, where so much of our lives are centered these days. That requires knowing their passwords.

FIRST STEPS

At the time of your loved one's death, it's likely they were logged into a number of accounts on their phone or their computer. **Do not log out of those accounts or turn off their devices!** Typically, their passwords are saved in each of these accounts. Ideally, you should find and reset them.

That may feel weird to you, as if you're invading your loved one's privacy, especially in the immediate aftermath of their death. But it's a real issue, and it's important.

After Mom was killed, my wife went over to her house and found that the laptop was still on with several tabs open—stuff my mom was apparently working on earlier on the day she died. Shutterfly was open because she was working on an album. My wife was able to request a password reset on the Shutterfly account, which was sent to her Gmail account. Her Gmail was open too, giving us access to her email, and we reset her password to ensure that we wouldn't lose it.

And of course, having access to your loved one's online accounts means that you can also close and delete them when the time comes. As we'll see, without their password, that can be difficult at best.

SOCIAL MEDIA

If you have your loved one's account information, deleting their Facebook page, say, is as simple as logging on. Facebook—and Instagram, which it owns—are among the social media platforms that also enable you to memorialize an account. That ensures that the photos your loved one shared are preserved and that their friends can still post remembrances on their page. But no one will be able to log in to the account, and it won't appear in public searches.

These policies may change with time, of course, and other social media platforms have different practices. As a general rule, they won't distribute passwords to others, regardless of relationship or circumstances. That means that without a password, you can't get into your loved one's account—period. No exceptions. That said, some platforms will delete an account if you provide documentation of your loved one's death. But others have no such policy; unless you find the password, the account will live on.

Some platforms allow the account holder to provide someone else access to their account if they haven't used it in 180 days, or some such period. In such a case, the person they'd designated would get an email giving them access to the account at that point.

> ### SOCIAL MEDIA POLICIES FOLLOWING A DEATH
>
> You'll find descriptions of how major social media platforms handle accounts in the aftermath of a death in Appendix 5. (You can find the same list with clickable links to the policies of leading platforms on my website, *KyleBachus.com*.)

EMAIL ACCOUNTS

Having access to the information that flows into your loved one's email account or accounts can be invaluable, however uncomfortable it may feel. Auto-billing notifications. Password reset instructions. Subscription reminders. Contact information for their friends or distant relatives. When you pause to think about it, it's remarkable how dependent we've become on digital services to manage our lives, express ourselves, and connect with others. Stepping into the online world your loved one created, if only to shut it down, has become a critical component of gaining some sense of control in the aftermath of their death.

CHAPTER 6

The Estate

When a loved one dies unexpectedly, the question of who is entitled to their possessions—or, put differently, how they wanted their possessions distributed—can arise almost immediately. Having an answer can prevent family problems from erupting at a time when everyone is already so deeply stressed.

The short answer is that if your loved one left a will, they dictate who gets what, from their real estate to their personal property, the clothes hanging in their closet to their animals. If they did not, state law dictates how their possessions are distributed.

My mother did not have a will; if she had, she could have made her own arrangement and determined where her cats were to go. She could even have set aside money to cover the costs of their food and medical care over the balance of their lives. If she had done so, it wouldn't have mattered where my sister, brother, or I wanted them to go, or on what terms. Because she didn't, the pets were legally our responsibility.

WHERE TO LOOK

The first step in handling your loved one's estate is determining if they had a will. In my mother's case, we weren't sure. So, where to look?

You may be able to find your loved one's will in a file or folder among their belongings. Start there.

If you know or can find the name of their attorney, contact them. If the lawyer sees your loved one's death notice, they may also contact you.

If your loved one had an attorney, they may have filed their will with the county probate court; an individual can do it too. So, check for a will on file. Once it's filed with the probate court, it becomes a public document.

WHAT MAKES A WILL VALID

In every place that I know of, a will must be signed by two witnesses and a notary public to be valid. The witnesses cannot be people who stand to benefit from the provisions of the will, either. If either of those conditions isn't met, the will isn't technically valid.

That said, you may find that your loved one has written a will but didn't get it signed and notarized. It looks like a will and smells like a will, but is it a will? In many states, yes. Lawyers call these "holographic wills." A probate judge may hold a hearing to determine whether such a will truly represents your loved one's wishes, based on factors such as what they may have said to others.

A second complication: your loved one may have written more than one will over the years. Life changes; your assets and your wishes can too. If multiple wills exist, it's the most recent that counts.

WHEN THERE'S NO WILL

If your loved one leaves no will, or if you cannot find one, then in legal terms they are said to have died "intestate." Every state has its own law to deal with these situations—and they're all different. These laws dictate how the assets of someone who left no will are to be distributed. They are long but generally easy to read.

Although these laws differ by state, they do share important commonalities. Generally speaking, they look first to whether there is a surviving spouse, and then to whether there are surviving children. If a spouse and children survive, the law may dictate varying shares; in Colorado, the first $100,000 of the estate goes to the spouse, and if there's anything left after that,

50 percent goes to the spouse and the balance is divided among the children.

If there is no surviving spouse or children, then parents are typically next in line. From there, different states' laws go in different directions.

As with a will, there are some assets—notably life insurance and retirement accounts—that fall outside the intestate succession law. They're distributed to the beneficiaries your loved one named.

My mom and dad were divorced when we were young. Florida's intestate succession law says if you die without a spouse and have children, even adult children, all of your possessions are split equally among the children. The word "equally" can be open to interpretation—that's one disadvantage of not leaving a will—and it's the probate judge who can settle any disputes over just what that means if you can't work it out.

YOUR STATE'S INTESTATE SUCCESSION LAW

You'll find a list of state laws on intestate succession in Appendix 6. (You can find the same list with clickable links to the actual laws on my website, *KyleBachus.com*.)

PROBATE COURT

Just seeing the word "probate" may make you nervous because of its common connotations: an expensive, time-consuming process and a very big deal. That is not necessarily the case. There certainly are complex estates that raise complicated, even contentious, issues that require a long probate process. But probate is a very common and—most often—straightforward legal process and often a necessary step in transferring the assets someone leaves behind to their beneficiaries.

If your loved one owned real estate—lawyers refer to it as *real property*—then a probate judge must approve any transfer of the property. If there's no real estate but the assets exceed a certain amount—it varies by state; in some, it's $100,000, and in others, less—then you'll have to go before a probate judge too.

If there's any reason within the family's dynamics that make it important to have an independent arbiter, it's worth choosing to go to probate court. If any heirs to the estate are minors, it's critical to go through the probate court process to ensure their assets are protected. That is because minors are considered incapacitated under the law: not legally ready to make and take responsibility for their own decisions. If minors are the sole heirs, I can't imagine a circumstance in which it would be appropriate for the adults in the family to go it alone.

One reason I say all this is to protect the adults. If you don't go through the court process and emerge with a judge's formal determination on how your loved one's assets and debts are to be handled, it's technically possible for a minor to reach the age of eighteen, turn around and sue the adults who took or spent money from the estate, transferred its assets, or sold possessions over the consequences of their decisions. Sound far-fetched? Let's say the grandparents took care of the kids and spent $10,000 on a swimming pool for them to enjoy. Any one of them could reach eighteen and sue, saying that was their money for college.

As with the criminal justice system, the probate judge plays the role of the referee. It's their responsibility to make sure the assets are distributed as the law requires and that any debts are paid. Probate courts are busy, and it can take up to a year to complete the process.

One decision you'll face is whether to hire a probate lawyer to help you navigate the system. If your loved one had very few assets, you may not need help. If the estate is large, the family's dynamics complex, or there's real estate involved, you probably do.

In any event, it's important to know that the cost of hiring a lawyer and going through probate are typically modest—more on the scale of a few thousand dollars rather than tens of thousands.

Small Estates

States have recognized that the full probate process isn't always necessary. If your loved one owned no real estate and had relatively few assets—again, it varies by state; in Colorado it's $70,000 or less—you can typically avoid probate court by filing what's called a "small estate affidavit." It's a simple document, often a form, and if you're in line under the law to receive some of the assets, you can sign the form and get it notarized. That will enable you to get access to bank accounts, sell vehicles, dispose of any other property, then distribute the assets as your state's intestate succession law dictates. You have a legal obligation—it's called a "fiduciary duty"—to act in the best interests of everyone involved.

Even in these cases, it can be helpful to get a probate lawyer involved, just to make sure you're on the right path under the law. If you don't, you could face liabilities or ill feelings down the road.

> ### SAMPLE: SMALL ESTATE AFFIDAVIT
>
> You'll find a sample small estate affidavit in Appendix 7.

WHO'S IN CHARGE?

If your loved one left a will, it typically names an executor who is responsible for seeing that their wishes are honored in the transfer of their real estate and possessions. If you're going through the probate system, the judge will issue a "letter of administration" to the executor, authorizing them to handle the estate's liabilities and assets.

If there's no will, the state's intestate succession law is going to dictate who's in control, and again, the probate judge will issue that person a letter of administration authorizing them to carry out their responsibilities.

If it's a small estate with no will, the person who signs the small estate affidavit is effectively in charge.

WHAT'S OUTSIDE THE WILL?

Many assets aren't controlled by a will. Instead, they're controlled by the beneficiaries your loved one designated when buying the policy or creating the account. The most significant are typically life insurance, bank accounts, and retirement accounts, such as a 401(k).

The benefit in this is that these assets don't have to go through probate. They're typically available to the beneficiaries—there can be more than one—much more quickly as a result.

Life Insurance

The whole point of a life insurance policy is to support those you leave behind. They can't be purchased without designating one or more beneficiaries. As with a will, locating your loved one's life insurance policy can be a challenge. Begin by checking their files. If that turns up nothing, you can check their bank account for evidence of premium payments they've made. It's also possible that the life insurance company will contact you—they monitor death certificates—but you can't count on that. It's best to be proactive.

Many employers also provide life insurance among their benefits. The amounts are typically modest—$25,000 or $50,000—or they may provide for a year's income. Again, be proactive. Reach out to previous employers to see if any coverage remains in place or, if they were in between jobs, whether they were on a COBRA plan.

Once you've confirmed the existence of a policy, reach out to the insurance company's claims department to report your loss. Generally, if you provide a death certificate, they will provide next of kin a copy of your loved one's insurance application. That's where the beneficiaries of the policy are designated.

As with a will, life insurance beneficiary designations aren't subject to debate—which can lead to its own complications. I know of one case in which a husband changed the beneficiary on his life insurance following a divorce from his now ex-wife to his brother. His intent was to support his two children, now living with his ex-wife; because they were minors, he wasn't sure how to do that. He could have named the kids as beneficiaries, and it would have been fine—but he didn't, and his intent didn't matter. After he died in a car crash, the proceeds of his life insurance went to his brother—who was under no obligation to share the money. His ex-wife could hire a probate lawyer and fight it out in court, but it would be protracted and messy.

You do not have to file a claim for a life insurance policy within a certain time frame. But when you do file the claim, benefits are generally paid promptly. That is because they are owed as of the date of death. In fact, life insurance death benefits will usually grow with interest until the claim is filed or until the life insurance company is able to locate the beneficiary to make payment, so it has every incentive to pay quickly. That would be true even if you didn't find the policy for six months; in such a case, the insurance company would owe you interest over that time on top of the benefit you're due. Generally, life insurance proceeds you receive as a beneficiary due to the death of the insured person are not taxable or included in gross income and, therefore, do not have to be reported on your tax return.

Bank Accounts

A jointly held bank account will pass to the other person whose name is on it regardless of what a will says. So will individual bank accounts with survivorship rights, in which the person who opened the account designated who it should pass to in the event of their death.

Individual bank accounts without survivorship rights become part of the estate.

Retirement Accounts

In opening a 401(k), Roth, or some other form of retirement account, many people designate their spouse as the primary beneficiary. When they die, control over the account passes automatically. They can also designate secondary or contingent beneficiaries; often, it's the children. In such a case, if the spouse has died too, the retirement account passes to the children based on whatever percentages the person who created the account established.

If the person who created the account did not name beneficiaries, then it becomes part of the estate.

Other Exceptions

Pension benefits, disability insurance, and annuities typically all involve designated beneficiaries. I'll cover all of these more fully in Chapter 9, but in this context, what matters is, if there is a beneficiary, they fall outside of the will too.

TRUSTS

It's possible that your loved one established a trust and transferred the assets that are normally covered in a will there. A trust is a form of estate planning that enables the person or people they designate—their trustees—to transfer their assets without going through probate court, regardless of the size of the estate or whether there is real estate involved.

If your loved one did have a trust, first, you are probably aware of it, and second, they have given you and their other loved ones the gift of a simpler, more straightforward process following their death.

As with a will, in the event of their death, you'll want to locate a copy of the trust document. And if you're a trustee, I'd still recommend that you meet with a lawyer—perhaps the one who prepared the trust, and if not, then someone who specializes in trusts—to help you understand your obligations and the steps you need to take.

INSOLVENT ESTATES

Let's say your loved one owned no real estate, and when you add up their assets and their debts, you realize that the debts are bigger. If that's the case, there's no need to probate the estate. In the next chapter, I'll discuss how to handle your loved one's bills after their death—but for now I'll simply say that if the estate is insolvent, you should *not* sign any documents indicating that you're going to take on responsibility for your loved one's debts.

CHAPTER 7

Handling Their Bills

Here's something particularly important to understand: when a loved one dies, even if you are among their heirs, you are *not* personally responsible for paying their debts. You don't owe their credit card debts. You don't owe their medical expenses, their utility bills, or their cable bill.

If your loved one's estate has assets, the people or companies that are owed money may have a claim against the estate—but it's up to them to take the steps necessary to protect those claims. If they do, that could reduce your inheritance. If they don't, that money is not owed—not by the estate and not by you personally.

In that sense at least, your loved one's death is not a financial burden. They may have left hundreds of thousands of dollars in credit card and medical debts as well as a stack of unpaid utility bills. You may be an heir to the estate or a close relative, but you are not personally responsible for those bills.

WHAT TO DO WHEN BILLS COME

What I've said begs a question: what should you do with your loved one's bills? I'm not giving legal advice specific to your circumstances here; for that, you can always consult with a probate lawyer. Instead, let me describe how my family handled the bills following my mother's death.

The first step we took was filing a notice with the post office to have her mail forwarded to my address. I did not have her mail forwarded in my name, because I didn't want her creditors putting pressure on me, but simply to my address. With that, her mail, including her bills, began to arrive at my house.

When a bill came in, I'd write a note on it saying that, unfortunately, my mother had passed away. That's all I put. I didn't put my name on it; I didn't say that I wasn't going to pay it. I included a copy of her death certificate along with my note on the bill and sent it back.

It's important for you to be emboldened to do the same. You don't owe the money; the estate may, at some point, but you don't. The smaller the bill, the more likely it is that you'll never hear from that creditor again. They will write the balance off at their end and move on.

If they persist and send more bills—and some will—just do the same thing: write the note, include the death certificate, and return it.

You should never make a representation that you're going to pay a loved one's bill. And you certainly should not feel obligated to do so.

APARTMENTS AND RENT

If your loved one was leasing an apartment at the time of their death, it's important to know that you are not personally responsible for fulfilling its terms—unless your name was on the lease. In that case, you would be responsible for continuing to pay rent. As is the case with other bills, the landlord could also file a claim against your loved one's estate for the remaining lease payments or any damage done to the property. It may also be worthwhile for you to review a copy of the lease to see if it explicitly voids any debts in the event of the tenant's death.

Practically speaking, we typically recommend that families approach the apartment complex, provide a copy of the death certificate, and offer to work with the landlord to terminate the lease at no cost. That involves working industriously to get your loved one's belongings out of the apartment and clean it up, just as they would have when their lease came to an end. Having done that, you can then turn over the keys and walk away. Under no circumstance should you offer to pay money; remember, you're not personally responsible.

You're much more likely to have the landlord make a claim against the estate if you abandon the property, failing to remove your loved one's possessions and clean up. In that case, you'd be leaving the landlord to face a significant expense in the absence of any communication from you. That is inviting a claim.

Generally speaking, we've found that landlords are not interested in chasing money through the probate process after a tenant dies. If you approach them, not with an offer of money but rather to leave the apartment emptied and in a nice condition by a certain date, they're likely to extend their condolences, thank you, and agree.

NOTICES TO CREDITORS

If your loved one's estate includes real estate or is large enough that it must go through probate court, you'll be required to file a list of creditors and the court will require you (or your lawyer) to send them a notice of your loved one's death. As more creditors become known, you'll need to send them notices too. In the meantime, as the bills come in, just keep sending them back with the same note in the same way.

Once notified, creditors are responsible for hiring their own lawyer and filing the appropriate paperwork to make a claim against the estate. Each state has its own rules about how quickly a creditor must bring such a claim; it may be as short as ninety days after receiving the notice. It's in your interest to send out these notices because, as you do, the clock starts ticking. If a creditor misses the deadline, their claim is waived forever. Period.

Most credit card companies choose not to pursue their claims. They know that a certain number of people they loan money to are going to die, and they're not about to participate in probate proceedings all over the country to recover that money. They write it off as a loss for the company, and they recoup it through the interest rate they charge other customers. My mother had several credit cards with a combined debt of a few thousand dollars when she died. Because she owned a house, we ended up in probate court. The credit card companies got their notices—and none made a claim before their deadline passed. As a result, her credit card debts were wiped away.

EXCEPTIONS TO THE RULE

There are exceptions to the rule, but they're at your discretion. Take utility bills for example. If you don't pay the electric bill, they're going to turn the lights off. In our case, we had to move a lot of stuff out of my mother's house before we could put it up for sale. So, we chose to pay the utility bills and keep the lights on.

You may also *choose* to pay some of your loved one's bills because it feels like the morally right thing to do. Medical care could be a case in point. I'm not saying you *shouldn't* do that, if you feel compelled to. My point is that it's your *choice*, not an obligation.

CHAPTER 8

Handling Their Property

Legally speaking, the property your loved one left behind may fall into two categories: real property, meaning any real estate they owned, and personal property, meaning everything else. Both have come up already, in Chapter 6, but there's more you should know about disposing of them.

REAL PROPERTY

Real estate is just like a bank account in one sense: if it's jointly owned, that property will simply pass to the survivor, most typically the spouse. That means if you jointly own a house and your spouse dies, you own the home. Real estate can also be transferred through a trust if one is in place. (We covered trusts in Chapter 6.)

If, however, your loved one owned their real estate independently, without a trust—as was the case with my mother—you are going to need to go to probate court in order to transfer ownership to someone else. This is the case whether there's a mortgage on the property or not.

If there is a mortgage, I do recommend being proactive in notifying the mortgage company of your loved one's death to ensure that you understand the remaining balance, the size of the monthly payments, and when they're due. A mortgage is what is called a "collateralized debt." That means the mortgage company has the right to be paid back in full upon the sale of the property; if you fail to timely make the monthly payments on the mortgage, then the mortgage company can take legal action to foreclose on the loan and force a sale of the property. Not the kind of thing you want to be dealing with if you can avoid it—and you certainly don't want to be blindsided by an unexpected foreclosure.

You'll have an array of options to consider. Are you going to seek to assume the mortgage and refinance to keep the property? Sell the property? Banks and mortgage companies have priority as creditors; technically, they're called secured creditors. They are going to get paid, and that doesn't change simply because your loved one has died. If you sell the property, the probate judge is going to make sure the check is issued to the mortgage holder for what they're owed; the remaining balance is an asset that goes into the estate. If there's a will, the money will be distributed according to its terms, and if there isn't, your state's intestate succession laws will determine the distribution. (We covered these topics in Chapter 6.)

Reverse Mortgages

If your loved one was at or approaching retirement age, they may have taken a reverse mortgage on their property. This essentially involves borrowing against the value of their home with principal (plus interest) all due only when they die or sell the property. It's essentially a gamble by the mortgage company; they're hoping your loved one dies or sells before the size of the loan, with all of the accumulating interest added on, has grown beyond the value of the house. That's why they're typically offered only to older people. The good news in this gamble for the borrower is that you're never obligated to pay more than the value of the home.

If your loved one had a reverse mortgage, the consequences for you as their heir can be disappointing. You're not going to find yourself underwater; again, the amount due on your loved one's death can't ever be greater than the value of the home. But you may find that even if the value of the property has increased substantially, the estate won't benefit much from the sale after the reverse mortgage is paid off due to the accumulating interest.

PERSONAL PROPERTY

Everything your loved one owned that is *not* real estate is personal property, and as we discussed in chapter 6, it's either distributed based on their will or the state's intestate succession law. There are some things to consider in disposing of these possessions.

Clothes and Charity

When the host of *Jeopardy*, Alex Trebek, died in 2020, his family donated fourteen of the suits he wore on TV and hundreds of accessories to a charity, so they could be worn to job interviews by people in need. In northern cities of the United States, coats are hard to come by, and so are warm winter shoes and boots.

I mention these specifics simply to encourage you to think beyond throwing away clothes or other personal possessions to the possibility of giving them away instead. It can be a way of finding some measure of positivity in your loss.

Many people take their loved one's clothes and other possessions to Goodwill because it's well known, and there's nothing wrong with that. But Goodwill supports itself by selling these items, and there are lots of people in need. So, you might consider all your options locally; you may even find that some charities will pick the possessions up. And of all possessions, donating clothes may have the most immediate impact.

Cars

My mom left a relatively new car sitting in her carport. I had no idea whether she had bought it outright or had a loan. We looked for the title but couldn't find it. We weren't obligated to pay the insurance on it when the bill came due—we covered bills in Chapter 7—but the car was an asset, and if we didn't pay the bill, we'd have no insurance to protect it.

All of which is a way of saying cars are a big deal, and disposing of them can be complex. If there is a loan, it's not unlike a mortgage in this respect: it's secured by the value of the car itself. The lender holds the title to the car until the loan is paid off; if you don't pay the loan, you lose the car. If you can't find a title, that is probably why.

How to figure out who holds the loan and how much is due? You can contact the dealership, which is typically identified by a logo attached to the back of the car. Look in the glove compartment for any documents related to the purchase that might provide a clue.

In my mom's case, we checked both places and found nothing—but she had a checkbook in her house. Her case was in probate, and I had a letter of administration allowing me to serve as her personal representative while the case was under way. I walked into the bank with her checkbook, death certificate, and my letter of administration in hand; I sat down with their representative and explained that I had no idea how many accounts she had held there, what was in them, whether there were any automatic withdrawals—and, if there was a car loan, who held the title. I had to go through a process and paperwork, but they printed out the last six months of her statements. I reviewed them and found a recurring monthly charge from a local credit union pulling out what looked like a car-sized payment every month.

The credit union was my next stop, where I went through the same process and learned the size of the remaining balance. We were able to reach an agreement for them to buy back the car.

And remember: as we discussed in Chapter 7, you're not *personally* obligated to pay off the car. If it's worth less than what's owed, just drive the car to the lender location and give them the keys, tell them where it's parked, remove the plates—and walk away. (It's not quite that simple, really; you should get some sort of acknowledgment that they took the vehicle, whether it's in writing or a photograph of the car with their representative beside it.) If the lender is owed more than the value of the car when they sell it, they're responsible for making the appropriate claim against the estate.

CHAPTER 9

Death Benefits

Your loved one may have left behind any of a number of death benefits that can help your family cope with the financial consequences of their loss. The most common is one you might overlook, so we'll start there.

SOCIAL SECURITY

We tend to think first of Social Security as the government's retirement plan, but that's actually only one of its three components. It can also serve as disability insurance, which will be important when we discuss coping with a loved one's catastrophic injury in Part 3. But third, and most important for our purposes now, is what amounts to Social Security's life insurance component.

If your loved one paid into the Social Security system through their working years—the length of time required depends on their age at the time of death—then Social Security may provide what are called "survivor's benefits" to help stabilize your family's finances. These are ongoing payments. They're not available in every situation, but they're available in many—including some that may surprise you.

ELIGIBILITY FOR SURVIVOR'S BENEFITS

Here are some of the instances in which Social Security survivor's benefits may be available to your family:

- If your spouse dies and you are caring for their children under the age of eighteen (adopted children, grandchildren, and step-children can qualify under some circumstances);

- If your spouse dies and you're over 60, regardless of whether you have minor children;

- If you're a parent over the age of sixty-two and were dependent on a child who dies; and

- If you are divorced and your ex dies, depending on how long you were married.

The bottom line: It's important, in the aftermath of your loved one's death, to reach out to Social Security to see if you qualify.

The One-Time Payment

Here's an additional Social Security benefit that, while almost insulting, is automatically provided to a surviving spouse: a one-time $255-death benefit. There is one qualification: you must have been living together at the time of your loved one's death. If there's no surviving spouse, an eligible child can receive the one-time, $255-benefit.

Finding a Social Security Number

You'll need your loved one's Social Security number for any number of reasons. The funeral home will put it on the death certificate and may use it to notify Social Security of your loved one's death, but you'll need to provide them with it. You may also need it to access your loved one's bank account, and of course, you'll need it to contact Social Security.

But what if you don't know it? It happens, maybe more often than you'd think.

The first place to go is the last place your loved one worked. Every employer in the United States is required to keep the Social Security number of every employee or freelance worker. (Assuming, that is, that your loved one wasn't working under the table.) Contact your loved one's last employer, tell them they've died and that the funeral home is asking for their Social Security number. The employer can look it up and provide it to you.

HOW TO CONTACT SOCIAL SECURITY

You can apply for Social Security benefits or learn about them on the agency's website:

www.socialsecurity.gov

It's an automated service, and you should expect to wait on hold, but you can also call Social Security's toll-free number between 7:00 a.m. and 7:00 p.m. EST, Monday through Friday:

1-800-877-1213

You can also go to your local Social Security office and speak to someone who works there.

Don't Delay

In the case of a catastrophic injury that leaves your loved one disabled, Social Security will back-pay your benefits to the date of the disability. But that is not the case with death benefits. If you wait six months after your loved one's death to claim your survivor's benefit, you'll lose those six months of payments.

And even if the funeral home has notified Social Security of your loved one's death, that does not automatically trigger a benefit. You need to be proactive.

> **The bottom line:** contacting Social Security soon after your loved one's death to see if your family qualifies for survivor's benefits is important.

If Your Loved One Was on Social Security

If your loved one was receiving Social Security benefits at the time of their death, the funeral home's notification may stop their monthly payments from coming. If there's a gap, or the funeral home doesn't report the death, the government will want to be reimbursed for any payments received after your loved one's death. If you are your loved one's personal representative, it's your responsibility to send the money back. One more reason to be proactive!

PENSION BENEFITS

If your loved one received a pension through their employer, it may provide for survivor's benefits, in which case they would have named a beneficiary. With the rise of 401(k) retirement plans, pensions have become less common, but they were, for many years, a primary benefit of employment and remain so especially for public employees.

DISABILITY INSURANCE

Many employers provide long-term disability insurance, and if your loved one was unable to work and on disability when they were killed, you may find their policy provides a death benefit. In fact, that is generally the case. Many people overlook this possibility because they assume disability payments end with their loved one's death. That is not always so, and in those instances, the policy should designate a beneficiary.

ANNUITIES

Annuities are a form of regular payments that your loved one may have received as part of a previous legal settlement. They may also have established an annuity as part of their retirement plan.

Some annuities are paid during life only, in which case there's no death benefit. The last payment to come would probably fall into your loved one's estate, and at that point, they'd cease.

But most annuities provide what's called a "right of survivorship." They're paid out over a defined period of time; let's say it's twenty years for our purposes. If your loved one died ten years in, payments will continue for the next ten years too. In such cases, your loved one would have designated a beneficiary when the annuity was established.

DIVORCE AND CHILD SUPPORT

It's common for divorce decrees to address how children are to be cared for in the event one of the spouses dies before the kids reach the age of majority, which is eighteen in all but a handful of states. This is often done by requiring both parents to acquire a term life insurance policy as part of the divorce agreement. (It could also be done through requiring a parent to provide for support through their will.)

> If your loved one was divorced and you can't locate their life insurance, the divorce decree is a good place to look. It's a public record, on file in the county courthouse where the divorce took place. If you know one of the lawyers involved in the case, you can also contact them.

It's possible that the insurance policy will still be in force even after the child has turned eighteen. Let's say your loved one bought a ten-year term life insurance policy at the time of the divorce, when the child was twelve. They turned eighteen six years into that term—but if your loved one kept paying the premiums, the policy would remain in force for four more years.

THE HARD REALITY

When all is said and done, all too often families that have endured a tragic loss are faced with a question that seems to have no answer: how are we going to make it? A loved one's death can tear a hole in the family's finances so big that their estate and the benefits we've discussed simply can't close it. There's no end to the questions, really. Who's going to pay the mortgage? Put the kids through college? Can we even put food on the table?

This is a primary reason why families often look to the civil court system, which I'll describe in Part 4, in an effort to hold the at fault person (through their insurance and sometimes their personal assets) or the company responsible for the loss accountable.

Working through the practical consequences of a loved one's catastrophic death can seem like an endless challenge, and it's certainly exhausting. Understanding the resources and benefits that can assist you can only help. You will make it! Things will get better. I know because I've seen it and experienced it too.

> If you've experienced the sudden death of a loved one, you can choose to skip Part 3 and move on to Part 4. If your loved one has suffered a catastrophic injury, Parts 3 and 4 will both be relevant.

PART III

Practical Challenges for Families after a Catastrophic Injury

You know my personal story by now: how my mother was hit and killed by a concrete truck while crossing a street near her home. My family is far from alone in suffering such a loss. But in my professional life as a personal injury lawyer, we encounter many more families who are coping with the catastrophic injury of a loved one rather than their death.

If that describes you, you'll find that much of what I covered in Part 1 applies to your situation too: the police investigation, the criminal justice system, and victim's rights. The same is true of the topics I'll cover in Part 4—on taking control and seeking

accountability through the civil justice system, as well as finding
comfort and meaning in your ordeal.

But in terms of practical challenges, a catastrophic injury involving a loved one raises its own problems and concerns. I'll address
them in this section of the book.

There's a potentially positive difference in your circumstances
too: the person you love is still here, among the living. It doesn't
necessarily make it better or easier in the moment or thereaf-
ter—but they're here, and thank God for that.

I'll also say this: while it, of course, depends on the nature and
extent of the injuries your loved one suffers, I am continually
amazed by the willpower I see in victims of catastrophic injury
events and their families and where it can lead, regardless of
how terrible circumstances may be at the beginning. There are
no guarantees. But where there is hope, there are possibilities.
The road ahead may be long, but I encourage you to remain
hopeful. In the years I have spent working with families, I have
seen some remarkable recovery stories. Commit to taking one
day and one step at a time, and in most cases, things will get
better. That doesn't mean life is ever going to be the same, but it
will still be worth the trip.

CHAPTER 10

Medical Decisions

The first questions on a family's mind after a loved one has suffered a catastrophic injury are almost always medical: what's the nature of their injuries, what's their prognosis and treatment choices, and when (or whether) can they go home?

At the heart of these questions, and one potentially even more pressing, is another one: given the nature of their injuries, is your loved one capable of making medical decisions or not? In the short run, they might not be able to, even in a case with a promising prognosis. They could well be in a hospital's Intensive Care Unit, unconscious, in a medically induced coma, or intubated to help them breathe.

If they can make their own decisions, of course, they should. (If you're worried about their capacity to make decisions and they insist on it, you should discuss your concern with their doctors.)

But what if they can't make decisions?

ADVANCED DIRECTIVES

The first thing the medical staff will want to know is if your loved one created what's called an advanced directive. You'll often hear it referred to as a "living will."

If you don't know the answer, you'll have to look in the same places you'd hunt for their actual will or a life insurance policy: their files, their desk drawers, and their safe. In many cases, you will find these documents in the same place. An advanced directive could also be filed with their attorney or their primary care doctor. If they were conscious when they arrived at the hospital and needed immediate surgery, the hospital staff may have asked them to complete an advanced directive before putting them under.

What an Advanced Directive Does

Advanced directives, also known as living wills, aren't cookie cutter—but in general, they serve to capture your loved one's wishes in the event they aren't able to make their own medical decisions. Their purpose is to spare family members the burden of making life-and-death decisions for someone else while in a time of turmoil and tremendous pressure. Advanced directives can't address every medical situation, but they should address the issues that are most important to your loved one. They're a binding legal document, just like a will. If your doctors have a copy of your loved one's advanced directive, they are obligated to follow it.

An advanced directive can cover issues ranging from what kind of pain medications your loved one wants or doesn't want to when they want doctors to stop trying to fix what's wrong.

A Designated Medical Decision-Maker

Usually—though not always—an advanced directive will also include a document called a "durable power of attorney for healthcare." It may go by a different name, but its purpose is to allow your loved one to appoint someone to make medical decisions if they're unable to do so themselves. They may even name a backup.

Put the documents together, and you effectively have a binding statement from your loved one indicating under what circumstances they want medical care to stop (or just the opposite) and, in all other circumstances, the spouse, parent, brother, sister, child, or whomever they want to make medical decisions for them.

A Designated Financial Decision-Maker

Someone who creates the first two documents may also create a third: a revocable living trust. In essence, it will appoint someone else to make financial decisions on their behalf if they become incapacitated. It may require a doctor to declare them incapacitated before taking effect, and once your loved one recovers, the authorization ends. But while it's in force, the person they've designated has the authority to access their accounts, pay their bills, and handle other financial matters that arise.

DETERMINING WHO'S IN CHARGE

If your loved one has prepared all these documents, bless them. But what if they haven't? Typically, the doctors and the staff at the hospital will work with the family to make medical decisions for your loved one. As part of that, they'll encourage the family to designate a decision-maker or decision-makers with whom they'll consult. Whether your loved one had an advanced directive or not, your interaction with the doctors and staff often begins with what's called a "family meeting"; I'll cover that in a moment.

It's also possible to go to probate court to have a judge designate a medical decision-maker on behalf of your loved one. Think of that as a last resort. It's always better to work together as a family if you can.

THE FAMILY MEETING

As soon as they are able, the doctors and staff responsible for your loved one's care normally gather what's called a family meeting. It may not happen until your loved one's condition is stabilized. And if your loved one is likely to be released quickly or transferred somewhere else, it may not happen at all. But if it hasn't happened within, say, twenty-four to forty-eight hours after your loved one is stabilized, I'd strongly urge you to request a family meeting yourself if you have any questions about their condition and the plan for treatment. It's especially important if there is no advanced directive to guide everyone involved.

A family meeting is a structured gathering. It's not typically held in the Intensive Care Unit or at your loved one's bedside. Instead, the meeting may be held in a nearby conference room. The leaders of the medical team will attend along with immediate family members who are adults. The caregivers will identify themselves, provide a summary of your loved one's situation and their medical recommendations, and assess your desire for information and how involved you wish to be. They will also answer whatever questions you have. If they don't ask, it's a great opportunity for you to designate a family member the doctors and staff should reach out to first and a backup. You can ask for their names and contact information—a number of specialists may be involved—and discuss who will be providing you with updates and choices to be made and how frequently.

It can be a difficult and emotional meeting, but it can also be very empowering. Without it, you'll be left watching as waves of people come and go as they care for your loved one, without any idea of what they're doing or the seriousness of the situation.

Maybe you'll only need one meeting. If your loved one faces a lengthy stay, maybe you'll hold one every week. Whatever the case, be sure to take notes.

QUESTIONS TO ASK AT A FAMILY MEETING

First, don't forget that caregivers are busy because they're trying to help other families too. They have their own emotions, and they're conscious of behaving professionally. Some may be more patient and warm than others. But they chose to do this work because they want to help families like yours. It's their job to be honest with you, and they want to involve you in the process to the extent they can. It may not always feel that way because their work can be pressing. But don't hesitate to prepare questions—and ask them.

- What's reasonable, from your perspective, in keeping us up-to-date?

- Assuming there's no emergency, can we touch base every (x) hours?

- If a question comes up at a different time or we don't hear from you when we're expecting to, is there a number we can call and someone we should ask for?

- What time do your shifts change?

- What time of day do you expect to be seeing our loved one?

- What rules do you have about how many people can visit and when?

- If it's particularly important for a family member to have time with our loved one, because the family thinks it might help, can you bend the rules if you need to?

- What services do you provide in terms of pastoral or grief counseling, and how do we access them?

- What should our medical expectations be between now and our next meeting, in terms of recovery?

CHAPTER 11

Finances

I've never encountered a family with a loved one who's badly injured whose first question was, "Well, how much is this going to cost?" They're worried first and foremost about their loved one, not the money, and that is how it should be. But at some point, the family or the loved one is going to start asking themselves how they're going to handle medical expenses. And with good reason; the cost of medical care, especially in urgent situations, can be extremely high.

HEALTH INSURANCE

If your loved one had private health insurance, then the question of paying their medical bills may not be quite as pressing. The hospital will take the insurance information and their billing office can explain what your copays and deductibles are going to be. With most plans, there is a total annual out-of-pocket cap on expenses. Once it's reached, most health plans pay 100 percent of further expenses. And in most cases involving a catastrophic injury, you might hit that cap in the first twenty-four hours of care. If paying your share of the costs is a challenge, the hospital will work with you. They're not going to kick your loved one out the door.

If your loved one is on Medicare or Medicaid, the hospital will accept their benefits. You may still face copays and deductibles, but their coverage will ease the burden.

If Someone Else Caused the Accident

In cases where someone else is responsible for a catastrophic injury, I've seen families withhold information about their own health insurance coverage. They weren't responsible for the injury, so why should they pay for treatment? Instead, they'll press the hospital to bill the insurance for the person who caused the accident.

My advice: use your own health insurance. Your insurer may have the ability to recover some of what they've paid later. But if you withhold information about your insurance or wait months to submit a bill, you may jeopardize your coverage. And you may find out later that the person you think should be billed doesn't have enough insurance to cover your losses—and you'll still be financially responsible for the medical expenses.

Legally speaking, it doesn't matter who's responsible for the injury that brought you or your loved one to the hospital. Initially, you are financially responsible for the care you receive. That is not to say you won't be able to recover those expenses from the at-fault person or their insurance company in the future. We will discuss that in detail in Part 4.

Auto Insurance

If you were in an automobile accident, you might also think that your auto insurance should cover your medical expenses. In most states, you can purchase an optional "medical payments" coverage for your auto insurance. These benefits may provide as little as $5,000 in coverage, and I believe they are best utilized to cover any out-of-pocket copays or deductibles you face if you have health insurance. In these states, the at-fault driver can be held financially responsible for your medical expenses, but that's a long-term prospect; you'll be responsible for paying the bills up front.

The hospital might prefer to bill your auto insurance if it provides medical coverage because they could be reimbursed at a higher rate. But again, you might prefer using them to cover your co-pays and deductibles. For that reason, I recommend giving the hospital only your health insurance information.

A minority of states—as of the beginning of 2021, the number was eleven, plus Puerto Rico—are "no fault insurance" states for automobile accidents. Their laws are different. In these states, your own automobile policy is the first, or primary, payer of car-accident related medical expenses up to a limit defined in state law. It's not optional; it's required. That limit may be as little as $10,000. This is the result of a well-intended but flawed reform movement that took hold in the '70s. At its peak, more than thirty states were no-fault states—but experience showed that the result was higher premiums for every driver because all of them shared in covering the costs created by the bad drivers.

The term "no fault" is something of a misnomer. Even in those states, you can sue the at-fault driver to recover medical costs beyond the limit imposed in the law as well as other damages. And my advice is the same: even if you are in a no-fault state, you should give the hospital your health insurance information in addition to your automobile insurance information because, with a serious or catastrophic injury, you will run out of no-fault coverage sooner than you think.

If you have questions about what your auto insurance might pay and under what circumstances, or whether to provide that information to the hospital, I'd suggest you talk to a lawyer about it first.

NO-FAULT STATES

Here are the remaining no-fault states as of January 2021: Florida, Hawaii, Kentucky, Massachusetts, Michigan, Minnesota, New Jersey, New York, North Dakota, Pennsylvania, and Utah. Puerto Rico has a no-fault law too.

Retroactive Medicaid

If your loved one doesn't have private insurance, isn't covered by military insurance benefits, and wasn't on Medicare or Medicaid at the time of their injury, they're functionally uninsured. Retroactive Medicaid may be there to support them.

Never heard of it? That's no surprise. The first time many people learn about it is in the hospital.

Retroactive Medicaid allows applicants who are eligible for coverage to receive Medicaid coverage for up to ninety days *before* their application. Hospitals want to get paid—as they should—and if your loved one is receiving care and uninsured, they may bring it up with you. If your loved one meets Medicaid's eligibility requirements, it will cover everything from their initial ambulance bill forward. No other insurance works that way. It's a safety net, providing a way for uninsured people who have unexpected injuries to deal with their medical expenses without being thrown into bankruptcy.

The ninety-day window dates back from the date of an application. You won't find out if you're approved right away because there's a review process—and you certainly shouldn't wait for the ninetieth day after your loved one's accident to apply. The sooner you learn if you're eligible, the better. If you think you may qualify you should ask the hospital financial or insurance department for help in obtaining these benefits.

ELIGIBILITY FOR RETROACTIVE MEDICAID

Retroactive Medicaid isn't for high wage earners, but many working people may qualify. In 2021, when this book was written, the base eligibility limit for the program was a monthly income of $2,400 or less. It can vary from state to state.

The hospital can help you understand the relevant earned income numbers in your case, based on the state where your loved one lives and when their injury occurs.

If your loved one qualifies, the coverage retroactive Medicaid provides is robust. It pays for outpatient services, lab tests, X-rays, physician visits, home health care, prescription medications, transportation, medical equipment, inpatient rehabilitation, and more.

SHORT- AND LONG-TERM DISABILITY INSURANCE

If your loved one suffers a traumatic injury and is unable to work, you'll want to consider all the options the family has for covering the loss of income. And of their options, the most substantial and timely may be short- or long-term disability coverage.

It's possible that your loved one purchased disability insurance on their own, through a company such as Aflac. But many employers provide either or both forms of disability coverage as an employee benefit and pay for it either in whole or in part. If your loved one is incapacitated and you've been authorized to act on their behalf, you can go to their employer's human resources department to determine if they have coverage.

Short-term disability coverage typically kicks in within a week or two after an injury and usually covers the first ninety days of being unable to work. It typically pays between 60 percent and 67 percent, or two-thirds of your gross earnings, either as determined by the previous year's W-2 statement or by the most recent pay stub. It generally includes overtime and bonuses in the calculation, although the specifics in all these aspects vary from policy to policy. Short-term disability coverage is typically triggered by a doctor's note indicating that you or your loved one is unable to work—so you'll need to talk to your loved one's doctor about whether they believe the policy's definition of disability has been met.

Long-term disability insurance generally works the same way and picks up where short-term disability leaves off: at ninety days. Some policies are limited to instances where you can no longer do your own job; others provide coverage if you're prevented from doing any job. Others build in time limits: twelve months if you're unable to do your own job, with coverage continuing only if you're unable to do any reasonable job duties. But if your loved one continues to meet the definition of "disabled" in their policy, long-term coverage will typically pay all the way to retirement age.

In my law practice, we see more employers provide long-term coverage than short-term, on the theory that families may be able to stick it out for some time at least. The employer may pay for long-term coverage as a company benefit while allowing employees to buy short-term coverage if they choose. Short-term coverage is typically more expensive because it's more likely to be used.

The bottom line: short- and long-term disability insurance can be a life preserver—and you may not even be aware that your loved one has coverage. So, check with their employer.

SOCIAL SECURITY DISABILITY INSURANCE

If your loved one doesn't have short- or long-term disability insurance, Social Security provides two programs that may help.

The first is Social Security Disability Insurance, or SSDI. You'll often hear people say that these benefits don't kick in until your loved one is unable to work for a year—but that's not entirely true. If your loved one is *expected* to be out of work for a year, they can apply for benefits and begin to receive them sooner. The application process does take time. But the important point here is that it's a program whose limits are often misunderstood.

You may also hear people describe Social Security Disability as a program for those who are permanently disabled. Again, that's not entirely true. We have clients on Social Security Disability who are going through a lengthy rehabilitation. It's going to take more than a year before they can return to work, so they're eligible; when they do return to their job, the benefits stop.

Social Security has its own definition of disability: "the inability to engage in any substantial gainful activity by reason of any medically determinable physical or mental impairment which can be expected to result in death or which has lasted or can be expected to last for a continuous period of not less than 12 months."[1]

It's a rather strict definition, and it's a legal definition, not a medical one.

How SSDI Benefits Work

Social Security Disability works in the same way that Social Security in general does: you have to have worked long enough and paid enough Social Security taxes to be eligible for the benefits. The more you pay into the program, the more you can get out of it—at least until you hit the maximum.

If you don't know where your loved one stands, they—or you, if they're incapacitated and you've been authorized to act on their behalf—can reach out to Social Security to determine if they're eligible for benefits and at what amount.

1 https://www.ssa.gov/OP_Home/cfr20/404/404-1505.htm

HOW TO CONTACT SOCIAL SECURITY

I first laid this out back in Chapter 9, but here it is again. You can apply for Social Security benefits or learn about them on the agency's website:

www.socialsecurity.gov

It's an automated service, and you should expect to wait on hold, but you can also call Social Security's toll-free number between 7:00 a.m. and 7:00 p.m. EST, Monday through Friday:

1-800-877-1213

You can also go to your local Social Security office and speak to someone who works there.

The Review Process

It can take between three to five months for an SSDI application to be reviewed. It's a long process, involving assessments by a medical and a vocational expert. If your loved one doesn't have short- or long-term disability coverage, and it looks as if they'll be unable to work for a year or more, get the application in. If they make a great recovery and can return to work sooner, you can withdraw it.

Note: If your loved one has truly catastrophic injuries, they'll probably get their benefits with their first application. It appears as if the system is set up so that only the worst cases are approved on the initial application.

The system provides an appeal process called reconsideration. You can file the documents requesting reconsideration for up to sixty days after an application is denied. That is when most people get their benefits. But if your request for reconsideration is denied, you can appeal to an administrative law judge within sixty days of that. It could be as long as eighteen months after the initial application before the judge hears the case.

Ready for the good news in all that? If you persist to the point of winning your appeal, the benefits are back-paid to the point where the disability began. You've just got to get to the finish line.

Some families choose to pursue all this on their own; others get a lawyer to help them. If you do use a lawyer, Social Security caps the lawyer fees at either 25 percent of your past-due benefits or $6,000, whichever is less. The lawyer can't charge you an hourly fee, and they're only paid if you get your benefits.

SUPPLEMENTAL SECURITY INCOME

If your loved one isn't eligible for Social Security Disability Benefits, there's a second program that's available as a safety net: Supplemental Security Income, or SSI. It's administered by the Social Security Administration, but it's not actually funded by people paying into the program. Instead, it's funded directly by the federal government.

SSI is designed to help people with disabilities and limited income and assets meet their basic needs: food, gas, water, electricity, and shelter.

It's not easy to qualify. But you can apply using the contact information I provided earlier in the chapter.

IF YOUR LOVED ONE IS INCAPACITATED

If your loved one has a long road to recovery ahead of them and is going to be incapacitated for an extended time, the family may need to ask a probate judge to authorize someone specific to handle the financial aspects of their life, including submitting applications for benefits. The same could be true for making medical decisions on their behalf. The probate process is there to help you handle situations like these. The person the court designates is typically called the conservator.

CHAPTER 12

Making Adjustments

What if your loved one doesn't meet the definitions of total disability we discussed in Chapter 11 and wants to return to work as soon as they can but needs some accommodations made there? What if they're a renter and need accommodations made in their apartment?

This is a chapter about making necessary adjustments to adapt your loved one's environment to their new reality, and I'll begin with their rights under the Americans with Disabilities Act, or the ADA.

Most people have probably heard of it, and they may think it's been around forever—but it was only enacted in 1990. It's basically civil rights legislation, extending the same rights to people with disabilities that have been around longer for race, religion, sex, and national origin. It covers all aspects of participation in society, including employment, public accommodations and transportation, and telecommunications. That's why buses now accommodate wheelchairs, and curbs have ramps at intersections. And the ADA also provides important protections in the workplace.

EMPLOYMENT

The ADA prohibits discrimination against people with disabilities in all aspects of their employment, from recruitment to onboarding to promotions and layoffs. If a worker with disabilities needs reasonable accommodations in order to perform their job—and requests those accommodations—the employer is required to make them. In this case, reasonable is defined as accommodations that don't substantially interfere with the employer's ability to run the business. This aspect of the ADA originally applied only to large employers, but now, it covers any workplace with fifteen or more employees. If the employer refuses to honor a reasonable request, the federal Equal Employment Opportunity Commission has the authority to require it. You can also hire a lawyer to take action to enforce your rights.

HOUSING

Many people live in apartments, and people with disabilities have protections in this aspect of life through a different federal law that was passed about the same time as the ADA: the Fair Housing Act of 1988.

The Fair Housing Act requires all apartment buildings constructed after March 1991 to provide features that make them adaptable for residents with disabilities. This applies to every ground-floor unit in a building that doesn't have elevators and every unit in a building that does.

But here's where the law stops and may cause confusion: saying that apartments must have features that make them adaptable is different from requiring landlords to *pay* for the adaptations when they're needed.

What does this mean in real life? That a landlord must allow you to put in an access ramp if you wish but is not required to pay for it. The same goes for adjusting the height of light fixtures, expanding the width of a doorway, or adding handrails to the bathtub. The apartment must be adaptable and the landlord must permit these changes—but they're *not* required to pay for them. What's more, the tenant is responsible for restoring the apartment to its original condition when their lease expires and they leave.

Obviously, all of this can be a burden. But if your loved one meets the definition of "crime victim" in your state, the Victim's Compensation Fund discussed in Chapter 3 may cover some or all of these costs. You might find that your loved one has an insurance policy that does too.

One more caveat regarding the Fair Housing Act: it applies only to buildings with four or more units. That means people who live in a duplex aren't covered, and neither are people who are renting a single-family home.

Common Areas

The ADA provides protections against discrimination in an apartment building's common areas because they're considered to be public spaces. The rental office is a common area. So are parking lots and breezeways.

LONG-TERM CARE

Recovering from a catastrophic injury isn't just about acute care in the hospital. It often takes time and effort. And if your loved one needs long-term care in an inpatient facility, it can be a financially scary prospect, even if it's only for sixty days. But they may need access to vocational or physical rehabilitation services and equipment that can only be found in a long-term care facility; they may continue to need support once they're home. All of this can be very expensive. Who's going to pay the bill?

Their private health insurance will usually cover these medically necessary expenses, and if they're on Medicare or Medicaid, it is usually covered too. They can apply for retroactive Medicaid, which we covered in Chapter 11. But of course, they may not be eligible. Figuring this all out and getting the necessary approvals can be daunting.

The good news is that, generally speaking, we haven't seen people forced to go without services they need. It may take some work to get there—through their private insurance, government insurance, or even sometimes through nonprofit organizations dedicated to helping people meet such needs.

The place to start is by identifying your loved one's likely long-term needs as soon as you can from the doctors providing their care. Then, you can begin to investigate your options. We've often found that the doctors who prescribe the care can also have staff that will help you locate the resources you need and how to get them paid for.

WHERE ALL THIS LEAVES YOU

The sad reality of a catastrophic injury is that your loved one's life may never be the same again, and neither will the family's. Their daily life and their ability to earn money may change forever.

But your loved one is still with you. And in many, many cases, I've seen people who've suffered catastrophic injuries, and their families do what seems, at the outset, undoable. It can be a test of resiliency—a very long tunnel. But in the vast majority of cases, there is light at the end of that tunnel. There is a reason to hope. You can find support, options, and opportunities.

Helping families recognize this—and seeing how far hope can take them—is one of the most gratifying aspects of my work. It all begins with taking control of your circumstances to the greatest extent possible, one day at a time. And that's where we're headed next.

If your loved one has suffered a catastrophic injury, you'll find Parts 1 and 4 especially relevant too.

PART IV

Obtaining Accountability for the Forever Consequences

As it happened, cameras at the intersection where my mother was killed captured all of it. I haven't watched it, but my law partner has. She pushed the button for the Walk sign, waited for it to change, and began to cross. She was halfway across the second lane when a concrete mixer truck made a wide right turn—and struck her. The truck weighed 43,000 pounds. The driver, sitting high above the street, never saw her, never hit the brakes. She died instantly.

When the accident investigators my law partner hired examined the truck, they found that the concrete company had installed an aftermarket device on top of the right side of the dashboard, partially blocking the driver's sight lines when looking down and to the right. Its purpose was to allow the driver to adjust tire pressure depending on the driving surface. The experts we hired say it absolutely shouldn't have been installed there and didn't have to be. We pointed its presence out to the police, and their analysis concluded that dashboard obstruction partially blocked about 75 percent of the driver's view when making a right-hand turn.

Within weeks, the company voluntarily agreed to remove the device from hundreds of trucks.

That would not be the end of our efforts to seek accountability for my mother's death from the company and the driver who we believe is responsible for it. Our family wants to ensure what happened to Big Sissy is never forgotten.

As I detailed in Part 1, we emerged from the criminal justice process feeling extremely let down by the results. Due to a police officer's simple mistake, the driver faced no consequences beyond a $180-traffic ticket. Our circumstances were unusual, but our experience was not; many families who have endured the tragic death or catastrophic injury of a loved one find that trauma compounded by deep disappointment in the criminal justice system.

But that need not be the end of their efforts to seek accountability or compensation for their loss. Neither does it prevent the family from finding something positive in their loss or remembering their loved one as something more than a victim.

There is the civil justice system, a realm in which the family—not the police or prosecutors—controls the pursuit of accountability.

We'll begin Part 4 by exploring the purpose of this system and how it works and close it by discussing another important dimension of coping with the forever consequences of what you've endured: the legacy of your loved one.

CHAPTER 13

Accountability

The financial and emotional consequences of a loved one's traumatic death or catastrophic injury are huge. So many expenses, so much turmoil, so much anguish—and all because somebody else made a decision that caused them great harm.

As we discussed in Part 1, the criminal justice system exists to serve society's interests, not specifically your family's. It fills an essential role, but it doesn't come close to addressing the totality of the consequences you may be facing. It's not designed to.

The civil justice system is. It's not an avenue that every family chooses to pursue, or can. It has its own strengths and weaknesses. And while it doesn't provide all the answers and there are potential downsides, risks, and limitations, it's important to understand the powerful role the family gets to play, what a civil case can achieve, and how they work.

WHO'S AT FAULT?

The fact that your loved one has been killed or injured does not necessarily mean you can access the civil justice system. Its purpose is to provide compensation when someone else has done something wrong.

If your loved one was the only one in a car, fell asleep at the wheel, and ran off the road, the result may be a terrible accident—but that doesn't mean that there is a civil case. There is only a civil case if someone else was responsible for causing the harm.

Fault matters, and it can get complicated. The classic example is a person who's killed in an intersection because someone else ran a red light. That's fault. But what if the person who had the green light was speeding? How do you balance the two?

The answer varies by state because the laws in each state can be different. But in the vast majority of states, you can bring a civil claim if the other people's fault is greater than your own. Some states—and Florida is one—have a rule called "pure comparative negligence." That means even if you are 99 percent responsible for what happened to you, you can recover 1 percent of your damages from the other person, even though they were only 1 percent at fault.

What "Fault" Means

When I say "fault," what does it mean, legally speaking? The technical term for it is "negligence": someone acting unreasonably under the circumstances. That is the minimum threshold for a civil case. It doesn't mean that they have acted intentionally, that they set out to hurt someone else. You might run a red light but had no intention of hurting someone; that's still negligence.

Running the red light was negligent because it was unreasonable. You should know better.

Back in Part 1, I talked about the importance of pursuing your own investigation of what happened and not relying entirely on the police. This is why. If you can't prove that the other person was at fault—through evidence at the scene, video of the incident, testimony from witnesses, or by some other means—then you may have no claim under the civil justice system.

DAMAGES

The fundamental purpose of the civil justice system is compensation for the losses you've endured that were caused by the negligence of others. The person responsible for your loss won't go to jail if you bring a civil case against them; that only can happen through the criminal justice system. But they can be held financially accountable.

Again, the specifics vary some by state. But generally speaking, there are three major categories of damages you can claim in a civil lawsuit.

Economic Losses

Here, we're talking about compensation for actual financial losses: past and future medical expenses, past and future lost wages, the medical equipment or ongoing care that your loved one needs, any modifications or accommodations to a home or automobile, and any other out-of-pocket expenses. Most states don't cap these damages; you're entitled to full compensation.

Non-Economic Losses

The idea of a civilized society is that when someone suffers at the hands of another, we don't seek compensation through revenge or retribution or take an "eye for an eye." Instead, we put a monetary value on the totality of the harm that has been caused. That includes valuing the non-economic losses, such as pain, suffering, grief, loss of guidance and support, loss of companionship, loss of enjoyment of life, emotional distress or inconvenience, physical impairment and disfigurement, among others. We all know that dollars can't truly compensate a family that has suffered a tragic loss; there is no number for what my family has gone through since my mother was killed. But as a society, we've chosen compensation over revenge—and it's the right decision.

Unfortunately, many state legislatures have enacted laws putting caps or limits on non-economic damages. I can't imagine that those politicians involved in the passage of these laws have ever experienced the senseless and unnecessary loss of a close family member caused by someone's negligence! If they had, they would know how insulting such a cap is compared to the actual loss.

When these caps were enacted—typically twenty to thirty years ago—the standard number was $250,000. Some have been adjusted over time for inflation. In Colorado, for example, the cap was set at $250,000 in 1986; it was $613,760 in 2021. Florida is an example of a state with no such cap. So, in Florida and other States without caps, you can recover whatever the jury in your case determines is the fair amount of compensation needed to equal the value of the losses suffered, although the judge does have the authority to reduce the amount if they choose.

Punitive Damages

The third form of damages—punitive damages, often referred to as "exemplary damages"—are intended to go beyond compensation. They are intended to send a message: to punish the individual at fault and discourage others from acting in the same way. Punitive damages are only available to punish intentional, willful, wanton, or reckless conduct. You can't recover punitive damages for conduct that is only negligent.

Many states also put a cap on punitive damages, and there are constitutional limitations as well. In the absence of a cap, most courts will consider punitive damages of up to ten times the total amount of the combined economic and non-economic (or compensatory) damages. Anything above that is likely to be considered unreasonable and maybe even unconstitutional. If you were awarded $100,000 for medical bills and $100,000 for pain and suffering, anything over $2 million in punitive damages, or ten times your total compensatory damages, is unlikely to stand.

Some states cap punitive damages at one-to-one: punitive damages cannot exceed the compensatory damages. And in many states, a portion of punitive damages actually goes to the government. Why? I suppose because it's the government, and that's what they do.

Wrongful Death Laws

Unlike the general principles of negligence, which apply broadly across the country, cases involving a wrongful death are covered by laws that vary in significant ways from state to state. It's complicated. State laws differ in terms of who's eligible to make a wrongful death claim and what damages are recoverable. Caps on damages may be different than in general negligence cases. In some states, only the personal representative of the estate of the person who's died can make a claim; in others, the surviving heirs specifically identified in the state's wrongful death law can. Generally speaking, that means the spouse, children, and in some instances where there is no surviving spouse or children, the parents of the person who died. In Colorado, the appointed personal representative of the estate of the person who died is entitled to bring a claim for medical and funeral expenses. Immediate family members identified by the state's wrongful death law can bring a claim for lost financial support as well as for non-economic losses such as grief and suffering, loss of emotional support, and guidance. If a parent dies, and they were supporting their children through their job, then the children are entitled to compensation for the money they would have received from the deceased parent had that parent lived a full life expectancy; they'd also be entitled to compensation for their grief and loss of emotional support and guidance.

The Colorado example is just that—an example. The important point is that you need to consult the law in the relevant state—which means where the death occurred—to understand what's possible. Your loved one might have lived in California, but if they died in an accident while crossing Kansas, it's the law in Kansas that applies.

WRONGFUL DEATH LAWS BY STATE

You'll find a list of wrongful death laws by state in Appendix 8. Don't feel as if you have to hire a lawyer just to understand these laws. There is only one wrongful death law in each state, and while it may be a little wordy, you should be able to grasp what it means for bringing a wrongful death case in your state. (You can also find the same list with clickable links to the actual laws on my website, *KyleBachus.com*.)

DEADLINES

When it comes to filing a civil claim, time is of the essence. It's not that you need to do it in the immediate aftermath of your loss; my point is that the deadline for bringing a case can vary with circumstances; if you miss it, there's no second chance.

Each state has what's called a "statute of limitations" for bringing negligence cases involving injury or death. If you don't meet the deadline outlined in the law, you forever lose your claim. That means you either have to have settled your case through negotiation, or you have to officially preserve your claim by formally filing a lawsuit in the correct courthouse against the correct people and entities by the deadline defined by law. For the most part, there is no wiggle room. Why? Because legislatures decided that after a certain amount of time has passed, a person or company responsible for injuring or killing someone else should be allowed to stop looking over their shoulder and move forward with a sense of finality. Evidence gets old, witnesses move on, and it's not fair for the responsible party to be haunted by the prospect of a lawsuit for decades.

Generally speaking, the timetable for bringing an injury case is longer than for cases involving death. That's because when someone's injured, it can take time to determine the extent of their injuries, the anticipated length of their recovery, and all of the likely costs. But in cases of death, the statute of limitations begins running as soon as the day the incident causing the death occurred.

As for the timetables themselves, the specifics are all over the board. Don't make the mistake of assuming the deadlines in your state are the same as another, and certainly don't rely on word of mouth or what you read on social media.

The State and the Details Matter

Some states have statutes of limitations as short as one year; for others, it can be as long as four. I'd say the average is about two years—but that's just a rule of thumb. Do *not* base any of your decisions on that.

Let me give you an example of how complicated this can be. Let's say you're in Colorado, and you're hurt in an accident caused by a drunk driver who's just left a bar that knew they were drunk and let them drive anyway.

The statute of limitations for bringing a claim against the driver is three years. For the bar, it's one year. The law also says you can't bring more than one case, so you have to bring all your claims against everybody at the same time. And that means your deadline is effectively one year.

Here's another example. Let's say you're hit by a municipal bus while crossing a street in Denver. Under Colorado law, you have to put the city or state government entity on notice of your intent to bring a negligence claim within 180 days. What about the three-year statute of limitations in cases involving a driver? It's not the only deadline that may apply when the government's involved.

You've got to first meet the 180-day notice deadline, and then you are still required to either settle the claim or file a formal lawsuit to preserve the claims against the bus driver and the municipality before the three-year statute of limitations deadline.

We get lots of snow in winter. Let's say someone doesn't clear the sidewalk, and you slip, fall, and suffer a catastrophic brain injury on private property. That is covered under a different law, and your deadline to bring a claim is probably two years.

One more example to drive the point home. Let's say the person who was hit by the drunk driver in the first example was only sixteen years old. Because the injured person is a minor, the statute of limitations for the minor's injuries doesn't start running until they turn eighteen. They get two years from their eighteenth birthday or three years from the date of the accident, whichever is the longer period. So, they'd actually have four years to file a claim because their options don't run out until they turn twenty. But…the medical bills incurred by the injured minor while between ages sixteen and eighteen are, legally speaking, the obligation of her parents, so the claim to recover those expenses from the at-fault person is actually her parents' claim (who are not minors), and their statute of limitations starts running on the day of the collision.

The same variables and considerations may apply in cases involving death as well. The key difference? As I've said, the statute of limitations in cases involving death are typically shorter.

And that's just Colorado. In Louisiana, you can't even sue a bar that served the drunk driver too much alcohol. They're not liable under the law, only the driver is. You need to assume that your state's laws are different.

The bottom line: it's extremely important to identify the deadlines relevant to your circumstances so that you don't find yourself losing your case before you even get started.

Consequences for Families

One implication in this is that you may need to be making decisions about pursuing a civil claim at a time when you're still feeling very raw and in turmoil over the loss you've endured. But you can be comforted by knowing that just taking the time to determine the deadlines in your circumstances does not commit you to actually take any action.

You can do a Google search for the statute of limitations in your state. But, as I've said, you need to be careful because there may be a nuance in your circumstances that makes all the difference— especially if the government is involved.

Your most reliable source of information is a skilled lawyer who specializes in personal injury and death cases and knows how to closely examine the laws in the state where the injury or death happened. Not a general practice lawyer; a specialist. They have to know the nuances because the stakes are high. If a lawyer takes on a case and doesn't file it within the relevant statute of limitation, then their case is lost, and they've committed malpractice. Most lawyers who specialize in this area deal with the nuances every day.

These aren't questions that the prosecutor in a criminal case or your victim's advocate can answer for you. They don't specialize in civil cases, and they probably will refuse to even offer their thoughts on the deadlines because they don't want to bear the liability for giving you incorrect information.

PRACTICAL LIMITS TO ACCOUNTABILITY

The person or company responsible for killing your loved one or causing them harm may be legally accountable for what they did, and the law may require them to compensate you. But there's a practical reality that may limit your ability to recover for your losses: if they're broke, you may get only as much as the automobile or property liability insurance that they carry provides. In the case of medical negligence, it's malpractice insurance. In any of these cases, it's a snapshot: how much insurance coverage did those responsible for your loss have on the day and at the time the incident happened?

When we're talking about catastrophic injury or death, in most cases the insurance available is shockingly inadequate. In Colorado, the minimum bodily injury liability coverage required on your car is just $25,000. That is a legal policy. There will always be people who buy the minimum coverage required, either because they don't think they'll cause anyone harm or they don't have any assets worth protecting. It's all they can afford.

When a client brings a case to our office, the first thing we look to uncover after we identify those we believe may be at fault is the total combined amount of liability insurance those responsible for the loss were carrying at the time of the incident. The next thing we look at is the assets of the person or the company that caused the loss. Will that be enough to cover the gap between the insurance policy limits and the compensation that's due? Maybe the driver only had $25,000 in coverage—but if they were on the job and driving for Amazon, that's a different story because Amazon is going to be responsible for their conduct.

Generally speaking, people and companies with more assets buy more insurance. They have more to lose. Most companies have at least $1million in coverage, and many have ten to fifty times that amount in combined coverage. But at the end of the day, if those at fault have minimal insurance and no assets, you're very unlikely to ever recover the full amount you're due for the harm they caused.

Let's say you sue a driver who ran a red light and killed your loved one, then find out they only have $25,000 in insurance. You say, "No, there's no way I'm going to accept that," and you take them to court. You might win a million-dollar judgment, and it's money they legally owe you. But in the end, it's a piece of paper. Their insurance will pay the first $25,000, and the person responsible for your loss owes you the additional $975,000. You can go after their assets, but if they can't cover what's due and are qualified to file for bankruptcy, they can hire a bankruptcy lawyer for a couple thousand dollars and shed their debt. A civil judgment is just like a credit card debt; it falls behind secured debts like a mortgage and a car loan in the hierarchy, so once those debts are paid, you may find there's nothing left. You've won—but in some cases, it's an empty victory.

That is why it's important to try to figure out as much as possible about insurance limits and assets as early as possible and certainly long before the case ends up in court. This may sound a little overwhelming, but for lawyers who specialize in this practice area, it's part of what they do for clients every day.

There are exceptions. If you drink and drive, then kill or injure someone, you can't escape the judgment against you by filing bankruptcy. You'll be liable for it for the rest of your life. The same is true in many states of felonious killing, which means causing a death by willful and wanton conduct. And of course, you can only file bankruptcy if you truly don't have the assets to cover what's due. Like many top lawyers, we've been successful in arranging ongoing payments from people who have assets but made the gamble to drive around with only minimal insurance. Still, in the majority of cases, bankruptcy is likely an option for the person facing a sizable judgment.

THE BOTTOM LINE

Seeking accountability outside the criminal justice system represents a meaningful opportunity for families to recover financially for their losses and their suffering—but those who pursue it need to be aware of the practical limitations that may impact how much they can recover. That said, pursuing a civil claim can be an empowering choice because, unlike the criminal justice system, the civil justice system puts the injured person or their family (in the case of a death) in control of the process. Next, we'll look in detail at how the civil justice system works.

CHAPTER 14

The Civil Justice System

I'm certainly not out to bash the criminal justice system, but the reality is that, in my mother's case, that system failed to deliver anything even close to the measure of accountability acceptable to my family. Let me restate the reasons I say that, pulling together aspects of her case I've discussed elsewhere in this book.

My mom was killed in a gruesome and terribly violent way. She left behind me, my sister and brother, our spouses, all of our children, her two sisters and their families—and a gaping hole in our family. The criminal justice system produced no charges against the company operating the truck that killed her and in the end only a $180-fine against the driver. And my mother was killed while doing exactly what she was supposed to do: crossing a street at the crosswalk, in broad daylight, with the walk sign. There's no ambiguity about what happened. It was all caught on video.

Then, our own investigation revealed that the company had installed an aftermarket device on the dashboard of its trucks that our experts determined left its drivers unable to see while making right-hand turns in urban areas.

From our perspective, the harm and the consequences didn't come close to matching up. My mother is no longer here to speak for herself, and the criminal justice system barely mustered a whisper on her behalf.

Fortunately, that doesn't have to be the end for us because the civil justice system is there too. It provides the opportunity to be heard—to have her heard—in a meaningful way that we can direct and control.

It presents the same opportunity to every family that has endured a loved one's tragic death or injury caused by the negligence of another.

THE TWO STAGES OF A CIVIL CASE

I don't want you to think that deciding to bring a civil case means that you have to end up in a courtroom in a public courthouse, with you and your family rehearing and reliving the gruesome details of your loss, then waiting for a jury to return with a verdict that you don't actually control.

It *can* mean just that. But the vast majority of civil cases don't end with a jury's verdict. They end in a private settlement at some point along the way but before the civil trial even begins. In fact, many are settled before a formal lawsuit is even filed. That's because a case can be built by your lawyer and presented to those at fault, their insurance companies and their lawyers for informal negotiations in a way that makes clear that, if the case is not fairly resolved, a lawsuit is imminent.

What does settling a case actually entail? It means signing documents agreeing to release the person or organization that is at fault and their insurance company from any further financial responsibility to you in exchange for a negotiated amount paid to you. In nearly every case, some aspects of the settlement are confidential—typically, at a minimum, the dollar amount of the settlement. It can be in the family's interest to keep the settlement amount private, if only to protect them from friends or distant relatives who make assumptions and ask for money. (Yes, that really happens.) For some families, confidentiality is acceptable; for others, it's not. It's always a matter for negotiation.

Depending upon the circumstances, a settlement is the preferred outcome for many families. It removes the risk of losing in cases where the events are in question, the significance of your loved one's injuries are in doubt, or there's an issue of comparative fault, as I discussed in Chapter 13, that leaves two parties pointing their fingers at each other. But even if none of these issues are in dispute, many families are able to achieve a settlement that demonstrates real accountability on the part of those at fault, avoids cost, time, and the emotional toll of going to trial—including the necessity of reliving the details of events in a public courtroom and having the value of your grief become a matter of debate. And If there's a company involved, a settlement may create an opportunity for you to insist on changes in their practices as part of a settlement that a judge and jury couldn't order.

What argues against an early settlement? Maybe the family doesn't consider a small insurance policy sufficient to balance their loss; perhaps they want to find out as much as they can about the facts and details of what happened before deciding whether to settle later. Filing a lawsuit will force the other people involved to give statements under oath. The very act of filing a lawsuit creates a public document that, at the very least, puts your allegations on record.

I'm not suggesting one way is necessarily better than the other. It depends on your circumstances. But I do think it's important to know that most cases end in a settlement, not a trial. I also think it's important to understand how the civil justice process works before making your decision.

The civil justice system serves to empower you in seeking accountability for your loss. I don't think anyone should make a decision about how best to proceed without fully understanding the opportunities and significant benefits, as well as the potential costs and risks it presents.

What Your Lawyer Can Do

A well-established law firm that specializes in personal injury law can put together what amounts to a trial preview of the case before a decision is made to proceed with a lawsuit or settlement. That may begin with an independent investigation to gather evidence from the scene. I discussed what that entails in Chapter 1.

They'll also assess the prospects for recovering compensation for your loss. Some states allow anyone who's involved in a car crash to send a certified letter to the insurance company of the person who caused the accident to determine their insurance coverage.

Your lawyer can also probe for any other insurance policies that might cover the event, including your own insurance coverage. They'll do what they can to assess the assets of the person or company responsible for your loss, through such means as property records or corporate filings. They'll consult with the medical providers and other experts they'd call on in court to understand what their testimony might look like.

Your lawyer should have the training and experience in counseling you on the best course of action. That's based on you as well as the case itself; a good lawyer will take into account your family's dynamics, needs, and desires. We find that people trying to make decisions about how to proceed consider a lot of factors, sometimes including their empathy for the person responsible for their loss. That's less often so in cases involving death or catastrophic injury, where the value of the damages are so high. In those circumstances, I strongly advise my clients to, at a minimum, pursue the claims necessary to recover from every one of the available insurance policies.

How Your Lawyer Gets Paid

The last thing a family caught up in the aftermath of a wrongful death or catastrophic injury needs is to start paying a lawyer $250 to $500 an hour to assemble and pursue a civil claim. In fact, families grappling with such a loss are more likely to have just been thrust by the event into their worst financial position, not their best. That's where the contingency fee system comes into play. I covered it briefly in Chapter 1, but it bears repeating here.

A personal injury lawyer considering your case is basically taking an educated gamble on its likely outcome. You don't have to come up with money to hire them. In fact, they'll also front the costs of an investigation, and they'll typically agree to absorb the cost of their time and the investigation if your case ends in a loss or if you decide not to pursue the civil case in the end. Instead of being paid on an hourly basis or requiring a lump sum retainer up front, they'll agree to get paid a percentage of the money they recover for you. The more they recover, the more they get paid. Your lawyer will provide a written retainer or fee agreement for you to sign that will spell out the specific terms in your case.

Based on nearly thirty years of work in this field, I'd say that nearly all catastrophic injury and death cases are handled in this way, on a contingency fee basis. Now, the fee isn't small. It's typically around a third of the money they recover. That reflects the risk they're taking and the time it can take to successfully resolve a case.

Typically, any money that's recovered goes to the law firm first. They take out their percentage, address outstanding medical or other case-related expenses, and pass the rest to the family along with what's called a settlement distribution statement that lays out the math.

FILING A LAWSUIT

Let's say that you chose not to settle your claim, for whatever reason. The next step in the process is filing a lawsuit and preparing for trial. As I discussed in Chapter 13, there are deadlines for doing so that vary by state and circumstance—and if your lawyer misses one, you'll lose your case before you even get started. So, with most wrongful death cases, it's important to file the lawsuit as soon as your lawyer's pre-trial investigation is completed, with the evidence gathered, the experts you'll need hired, and how you intend to present the case thought through. Your lawyer will help you determine how much to seek in damages.

With a catastrophic injury case the deadlines for filing are usually longer. That's because it may take months or even a year or more for the medical recovery to reach a point where the future consequences can be accurately predicted. Because you only get to file one case, you want to be in a position to understand and seek to recover payment for all of the future losses related to the injuries. You can't really do that without having an accurate picture of what the future is likely to hold in terms of medical costs and wage loss.

In a catastrophic injury case, if deadlines permit, your lawyer will usually wait until your loved one is medically stabilized and has reached a plateau in their recovery before filing a lawsuit. In the legal world, it's called "maximum medical improvement." There may still be a need for ongoing medical care, but you're hoping to wait until the doctors know what your loved one's problems are, whether they are permanent, and what their chances of long-term recovery are likely to be.

Once a lawsuit is filed, the court system takes control of the timetables. It will impose deadlines to keep the case moving, including defining how much your damages are. If you file your case before you know the answer, the court system may not wait for you to pin down your future expenses. And that means your claim may fall short of your needs.

The bottom line: it's not always possible to put yourself in the best possible position before filing a lawsuit, because of the deadlines you face to bring your case. But it should always be the goal.

FIRST STEPS

Filing a lawsuit used to involve going to the courthouse and submitting the document in person, but now, it's almost always done electronically. When it comes to filing a lawsuit, that means the courthouse is effectively open twenty-four hours a day.

The next step in the process is still old school: a sheriff's deputy or a process server will deliver a printed copy of your lawsuit to the people you're suing. If there's more than one defendant, they'll deliver a copy to each of them. The defendant is likely to turn it over to their insurance company—it's what they should do—and the insurance company will deploy their own lawyers to defend the case. That means that, generally speaking, if the person you're suing has insurance, they're not paying the lawyers. Their insurance company is.

The lawyer hired by the defendant's insurance company has to formally join the case—that's called "entering an appearance"—and will face an initial deadline to respond to each of the paragraphs, or allegations, in your lawsuit. That response is called an "answer."

They'll respond to each numbered paragraph or allegation in one of three ways:

1. They can admit that what's asserted in the paragraph is true.
2. They can deny that it's true.
3. They can say they can't answer yet because they don't have enough information.

Again: if there's more than one defendant, they each have to file their own answer.

Everything they admit to is over, as far as the case is concerned. Everything they deny or say they can't answer yet forms the framework of what you'll argue out in court. We find that most defense lawyers will always choose options two or three because they don't want to admit anything at the very beginning of a lawsuit. They might not even admit to an allegation that the accident occurred on a certain date, saying they don't yet have that knowledge.

This can be upsetting to families, who expect the defendant to admit things they know to be true. But it's a common tactic because once defense lawyers have admitted to anything, it is very hard for them to take it back.

Once all the defendants have submitted their answers, your lawsuit is considered—in legal terms—to be "at issue." Generally speaking, at that stage, the judge will typically call an initial meeting with the lawyers from all sides in which the judge will lay out their plans for managing the case. This is often referred to as the initial case management conference.

THE JUDGE'S ROLE

As in a criminal case, the judge is effectively the king or queen of a civil lawsuit as it moves forward. Once a judge is assigned to your case, they take on the role of an impartial participant, the umpire of disputes, and the director of the process as it unfolds. But as a general rule, when a case actually goes to trial, it's the jury that decides the disputed issues and gives the verdict.

THE DISCOVERY PROCESS

The next stage in the case is the discovery process. That is the formal name for the period in which both sides get to discover as much as they can about the other side's case.

The Written Side of Discovery

Rules vary from state to state, but discovery typically begins with an exchange of written questions that have to be answered under oath. Those are called "interrogatories." If you bring a civil lawsuit, you're very likely going to have to answer the other side's written questions. Because the answers are given under oath, they can be used in court as if you were sitting there on the witness stand, giving testimony.

If written questions are the first tool lawyers use in the discovery process, requests for documents are the second. They're called "requests for production." In an injury case, for example, the defense will ask for all the medical records and bills resulting from the incident. In a case like my mom's , we would ask for documentation about who made the decision to put aftermarket devices on the dashboards of their concrete mixer trucks, as well as the driver's history and the training he received.

A third tool in the process is what's called a "request for admissions." That's a formal request to which the other side must reply. Your lawyer might send a formal request to the defendant to admit that they were the sole cause of the accident. If they do, that response is binding for the duration of the case.

In some states, and in all federal cases, there's an automatic requirement to disclose certain information at the start of the case, rather than requiring the other side to ask.

The Oral Side of Discovery

The oral side of the discovery process, which comes next, is a huge part of a civil case. These involve answering questions from the other side's lawyers, under oath, with a court reporter and maybe a video camera recording every word that's said. This is what's called a "deposition."

In a criminal case, which I covered in Chapter 2, the defendant cannot be required to testify in court. It's a constitutional protection. But a civil case is different: even if a participant in the case doesn't want to answer questions under oath, they can be subpoenaed to show up for questioning at a deposition. In most states, there is a limit on the length of time they can be forced to answer questions.

> ### A TERM YOU MIGHT HEAR
>
> A subpoena is a document that a lawyer can issue to require someone to give testimony or produce documents in a deposition or in court.

One thing a family has to consider is that if they bring a civil lawsuit, those who are claiming damages are probably going to be asked to give deposition testimony. The tradeoff is usually worth it because the right to demand depositions from the defendants and witnesses can be a very empowering tool for a family that's seeking answers. The person responsible for their loss can be compelled under oath to explain what happened. A supervisor or coworker of the defendant who may not want to voluntarily come forward with information can be compelled to answer questions.

At a deposition, the lawyers from both sides are present. They'll ask the questions, and if their client is on the receiving end, they can object to certain questions if the rules governing the process permit it. But in a deposition, most objections do not prevent the witness from being required to answer the question. It simply puts the objection on record for the judge to consider later at trial.

What if someone refuses to answer questions in a civil case? For defendants, it can be held against them. The judge will instruct jurors to assume that their answers would not have been in their best interest. A judge can also hold anyone else who refuses to answer questions in contempt of court, and they could face jail.

The Costs of Discovery

The discovery process isn't triggered until you actually file a civil lawsuit—and it can be expensive. The average cost of a deposition, once you've paid for the court reporter, the videographer and the deposition transcript, is on the order of $1,000. If you have a lawyer who's working on a contingency fee, they'll front the cost. But they'll recover their expense out of any compensation you're awarded, on top of their contingency fee. (Think of it like parts and labor for a car repair. The costs cover the parts, and the labor covers the work to install them.)

The total estimated cost of bringing your civil case to trial should be one factor you consider in deciding whether to settle your case or proceed. Your lawyer should be able to provide an estimated range of the total potential costs involved.

The Cost of Experts

The most expensive part of a civil case is the experts your lawyer hires to assess the circumstances of the crash or incident that led to your loss and the resulting damages.

Your lawyer may have retained a professional engineer or accident reconstructionist to determine the chain of events that led to your loss and who was at fault. They may hire an economist to calculate future lost wages with a rigor that makes the figure admissible in court or a forensic accountant to testify about your loved one's lifelong lost earnings and what each family member would have received. A vocational rehabilitation expert might be retained to explain the costs and process involved in retraining the person who's been injured.

In a case involving injury, one or more of the medical care providers are also going to have to testify. Many of their opinions can be obtained from medical records, but your lawyer will still need to meet with them because if the case ends up in court, the doctors will need to testify regarding the reasonableness of their treatment, what caused the need for the treatment, and their medical opinions about what the future likely holds. A brain surgeon or an emergency doctor is interested in practicing medicine, not testifying in court, so they might charge $1,000 an hour just to meet with them. After all, they can't be seeing patients or performing surgery when they're meeting with your lawyer.

All of these experts can be very expensive. And if they were retained specifically to testify in the case, they'll typically be required to provide a written report of their opinions to be disclosed to the other side—who, after all, may have retained their own accident reconstructionist, say, to explain the driver's conduct or assert that someone else was at least partially responsible for what happened too. Preparing such a report can cost several thousand dollars. Again, the good news is that the law firm you retain should be advancing these costs on your behalf. Your family will not have to pay for the experts out of pocket. The lawyers will get reimbursed out of the final settlement.

THE DISCOVERY CUTOFF

Once the expert opinions have been shared, that triggers a second round of depositions—because now each side is questioning the other's experts under oath.

But at some point there's a deadline, a discovery cutoff date ordered by the judge, in which everything you're going to present in court has been disclosed to the other side, and vice versa.

The discovery period can be as short as six months in some places and as long as a year or more in others. It takes time. When someone sends you written questions, you have thirty days to answer them; there's a month right there. Once the discovery period has ended, the case is ready to proceed to trial.

In some states, the judge sets a trial date at the beginning of the case; in others, they wait until discovery has been completed before setting the trial date.

PRESSURE TO SETTLE

Even after a lawsuit is filed, the vast majority of cases are settled short of a trial. And there's a good reason for that. By the time you reach the discovery cutoff, both sides have a very clear picture of who's going to testify and what they're going to say. You're not likely to learn any more new facts after the discovery cut off date. That leads to resolution.

There's nothing that says you can't negotiate during the discovery process. In fact, it happens all the time.

What's more, nearly every civil trial judge in America now requires both parties to sit down with a mediator before going to trial. The mediator could be a retired judge or a lawyer who specializes in settlements and serves as a neutral player. The trial judge will wait until the discovery process is near or at its end, so both sides know as much as they can about the other's case, and they'll force a settlement conference with a mediator.

A civil trial typically takes a week or more. They can be presented to a judge, but typically, they'll involve a jury. It's a big
event. It takes a lot of work to orchestrate and a lot of time in
the courtroom. And courts are busy.

As a result, in essence, trial judges are saying this: "You're not
going to come into my courtroom and consume a week of my
time unless you've made a real effort to get this case resolved.
I'm ordering a settlement conference. You, the plaintiff, and you,
the defendant, need to have your lawyers pick a retired judge to
preside and split the costs. If you can't reach an agreement on
that, I'll appoint the mediator. Your clients and your lawyers are
all going to attend. And you're going to sit down together for a
half-day or a day and see if you can get this case settled. And
then, you're going to report back to me. If you report that you
tried in good faith to settle but couldn't do it, *then* I'll let you
come try your case in my courtroom."

Civil lawsuits didn't always work this way. They used to be
more trial by ambush, with a less vigorous discovery process.
The change is deliberate. By ensuring that the vast majority of
evidence is understood by both sides before a trial, the current
process allows both sides to assess the strengths and weaknesses
of their case. You and your lawyer have an opportunity to discuss
what's in the family's best interest and the risks you're willing to
take—because, after all, the trial itself remains an unknown. It's
a public process too, an open proceeding that yields a record that
anyone who walks in off the street can see.

Based on my experience, I'd estimate that 70 percent or more of
cases that go into the mediation process settle in that meeting
or within a week or two afterward, as the two sides resolve their
final differences.

In total, if you look at all civil claims nationally, less than 2 percent actually end up going to trial.

THE TRIAL

Let's say you're one of the 2 percent who don't settle and choose to go to trial instead. I don't know of a better or more fair system than ours—because it literally puts the decision in the hands of regular citizens from different paths of life and different perspectives too. I think it's a beautiful system, the best in the world.

But at the same time, it's more than a little scary. There's so much you can't control.

The Jury

There's a common misperception that lawyers pick the jury. We don't.

It's the first step in a trial: the court calls a random selection of citizens to jury duty, and when they show up, they're assigned to a particular courtroom. It's literally a lottery.

Let's say forty people are called as potential jurors on the day your trial begins, and twelve find themselves in the jury box inside your courtroom. The judge might limit the lawyers for both sides to asking questions of potential jurors for half an hour each. This amounts to a bit more than two minutes of questions apiece. Then the judge will ask each side to eliminate three jurors. So long as your choices aren't racially driven, you're free to eliminate whoever you want.

The six people left in the box form your jury.

The numbers can vary. Some states sit twelve jurors on a case; others have six, eight, or nine.

In some states, the jurors in a civil case have to be unanimous in their decision. In others, it might be nine out of twelve. In still others, it might be a different measure for a majority. It runs the gamut.

The bottom line: the jury is one of the big risks in going to trial. You don't know who's going to show up for jury duty or what their experiences might have been.

The Proceedings

Because of the discovery process I've described, there are generally few surprises in terms of the evidence presented in the trial itself. But a trial is a live event. You never really know what a witness may say under pressure while on the witness stand until it actually happens. (I told you it was scary.) The plaintiffs present their witnesses first, and the defense gets to question them too. Then, the defense presents its witnesses, and the plaintiff's lawyers get their turn to ask questions. It can be a painful process for the family and for the defendant too.

As I've said, a civil trial typically takes about a week to unfold—but a complex case involving multiple defendants and contentious details can go on for longer. Unless the judge calls the lawyers in for a private conference, it all plays out in public. Every word is also captured in real time by court reporters, and the transcript becomes a public record too.

The Verdict

Remember, while the judge serves as umpire and instructs the jury, the people sitting in that jury box are going to listen to the testimony, retire to a jury room, consult a list of instructions, and arrive at a verdict. They'll fill in a jury verdict form, return to the courtroom, and present it to the bailiff, who'll hand it to the judge to be read.

There's always a pregnant pause after the judge reads the form, then looks over at the jury.

"Is this your verdict?"

"Yes, your honor. It is."

Did you prevail? Everybody will find out at the same time.

As I said: the best system in the world but scary. As a lawyer, my biggest fear for the families I represent is that I don't want them to be revictimized by a trial's outcome. It keeps me up at night.

THE OUTCOME

It can be a gratifying, even exhilarating, moment for the family to hear a jury find the person responsible for their loss guilty of negligence in one form or another and impose damages in compensation. What's happened to you has been heard; there's an acknowledgement you've been wronged and that life will never be the same.

But the result can also be more nuanced—and less gratifying. Perhaps the jury went to questions of comparative fault and decided your loved one was partially responsible for what happened too. The jury could award less in damages than you know to be necessary for your loved one's long-term care.

The disappointment can be crushing. Nothing seems fair, nothing seems right, your loss is real, and the world seems turned upside down—all because the jurors in the box, for whatever reason, don't see the circumstances the way you and your lawyer do. It happens.

In my experience, disappointments most often arise out of questions of comparative fault in cases where the circumstances are ambiguous. In Colorado, if it's fifty-fifty as to who's at fault, as a matter of law, no damages are awarded at all. The defendants might have a $10 million-insurance policy, but if the jury comes back fifty-fifty, it's a zero verdict for the family that might have lost a loved one. That's the law in Colorado.

THE JUDGE'S POWER

A judge has the authority to reduce the amount awarded by a jury if it goes way beyond what the judge believes to be reasonable, given the facts of the case. This is called a "remittitur." It's rare, but it occurs.

The risk in a trial lies on both sides. The defendants have the same concerns as you do. They might have settled a case for $1 million—only to go to trial and have the jury award $10 million in damages.

AN APPEAL

From the day that you file your civil lawsuit to the moment that a jury comes back with a verdict, the judge makes dozens of decisions along the way. You'll remember that I described the judge as the umpire in your case. Consider how many balls, strikes, and outs the umpire calls in a baseball game. Imagine there's a video of every pitch and a transcript of every call the umpire makes—and that the losing team got to pick every single decision the umpire made that they thought was wrong and appeal it to a panel of three senior umpires. If those senior umpires decided there were enough bad calls to affect the outcome of the game, they could throw out the result and order it to be replayed.

That is the essence of the appeals process following a trial. Every decision the judge makes is recorded, as is every word they say in court. The losing side has an automatic right to appeal any or all of those decisions, arguing that they caused an unfair trial. That process can take a year or more.

Does an appeal happen every time? No. But the bigger the amount you win by, the more likely it will.

WHAT IT ALL MEANS FOR FAMILIES

The goal of the civil justice system is to put families who have lost a loved one to traumatic death or catastrophic injury in a position to recover money damages for their harms and losses and hold the responsible person or company accountable for what they've done. It also permits the family to be heard and to obtain answers to questions about what happened and why.

More than any other aspect in the aftermath of a tragic loss, the civil justice system gives families control. Not over the result, necessarily. The family is only one part of the equation.

But it does provide families with control over whether to initiate the process and how far to take it. Remember: most cases settle, in part because avoiding a trial spares the family from reliving a private trauma in a public way. And a settlement can provide the family with certainty in terms of holding those at fault s financially accountable.

Ultimately, however, if the defendants compel the family to go to trial, or the family chooses to do so, the system provides for all sides to be heard and a final determination to be made. It happens every day.

Can it, in any real sense, make things whole again? No. Life is changed forever. But for the family, life goes forward—and, in cases involving injury, life will move forward for the victim too. That's what makes coping with your grief and finding some measure of meaning in your loss so important to many families. We'll take those topics up next.

CHAPTER 15

Rising through Grief

In the immediate aftermath of unthinkable loss or catastrophic injury, you can feel overwhelmed with shock, uncertainty, and anger. It all seems so senseless, unnecessary, and traumatic. For a time, trying to get through the next hour, and then the next day, and then the next week may be all you can manage.

The emotions you're feeling are real. Grief is normal—it's important to know this—though everybody responds to it differently. That's important to know too. There's no right or wrong way to experience grief, and we shouldn't judge how others express their grief. But as I've learned from my practice and personal experience, it can be debilitating.

My family was fortunate to have a friend who's a psychiatrist. She reached out a few days after my mom was killed to see how we were doing. She's not a grief counselor, but she referred us to one, and she pointed me to a book that I found so helpful I'll recommend it to you as well: *It's OK That You're Not OK* by Megan Devine. It's a straightforward and practical guide that was instrumental in helping me understand what I was going through. I've since provided a copy to almost every family I work with who finds themselves in similar circumstances, and a number of them have reached back out to me later to thank me for it.

I began to see the grief counselor too, and I've remained in counseling once a week for the last year. I've found that to also be instrumental in dealing with my loss. My wife and children have seen therapists as well, and they've benefited from the experience as I did.

I stress seeking help for your grief because I've learned how important it can be. The hardest part is just starting. We can all guess at what counseling might be like and whether we think it would help; my advice is to try it because if you don't, you'll never know the answer.

The great news in this is it's almost certain you'll find resources available to pay for counseling. To my knowledge, every Victim's Compensation Fund will pay for it. Victim's advocates in the police department or the prosecutor's office can usually refer you to free counseling services. You may find community-based nonprofit counseling services available too. In Denver, the former Broncos quarterback Brian Griese started a nonprofit called Judi's House—named in honor of his mother, who died of cancer when he was twelve—that provides free counseling services to children between the ages of three to twenty-five who have experienced the death of a family member.

The path through grief begins with regaining some sense of control over the uncontrollable that has befallen your family. You can't change what's happened; you can't bring back someone who is gone. You can't go back to the day before a catastrophic injury. But you *can* choose how to move forward. In fact, you have to, whether you consciously make a choice or not. Every morning when you wake up, you'll make the choice again.

So, what are some ways you can choose to move forward, for your sake and the sake of your family, in a way that honors the life you can't bring back or return to what it was before an injury? Whether it's for one hour or one day, what can you do to control what happens next?

Through the families I've met in my practice and the experience of my mother's death, I've learned that the answers can begin with small steps and needn't necessarily go beyond them. Simple things matter.

Walking Gently

Working through grief is not a straight path. You may be angry, withdrawn, or sad. And yet, here is the world going on around you as if nothing had changed—at the gas station, the grocery store, in the workplace, or wherever you need to be. It can seem as if others are all experiencing the rainbows and sunsets of life—and you're not.

Then again, you're also not wearing a sign on your chest as you walk into the grocery store that says, "My mother was killed yesterday." And of course, neither is anybody else.

With that recognition comes a new awareness that can rise out of loss: don't ever take for granted what's happening in other people's lives. Don't assume you're the only one who's reeling, who's suffering in one way or another. We can't know what others are experiencing. So, perhaps it's best to be a little kinder in our interactions with the people we encounter.

That's one choice you can make: to walk more gently through the world.

Cherishing the Day

Life is short. Tomorrow isn't guaranteed. We hear things like this all the time. But on the other side of an unexpected loss, we have a new appreciation for the reality in those words.

And if there is no guarantee of tomorrow, how do you want to spend today?

When a loved one is killed or catastrophically injured, there may have been a lot of things on their bucket list that they never got to check off. There may have been things they loved to do that put a smile on your face whenever they come to mind. One way to honor their memory is to complete that bucket list or do some of the things they loved to do.

That's a second choice you can make: to cherish the day, perhaps in ways that they might have cherished too.

CHAPTER 16

Legacy

My mother was the first woman to graduate from the University of Florida with a Master's Degree in Fine Arts in Theatre. It was something she was very proud of, and we're very proud of it too. She was managing a home with three kids when she pursued her passion for the arts and went back to school, graduating in 1977 with her Master's in Theater Directing.

Mom's trailblazing didn't stop with her degree. She became an advocate for women in general and for the fine arts. She acted professionally. She started a children's theater, writing, directing, and touring throughout the state of Florida. And she went on to work as a writer and director for the Universal Studios theme parks in Orlando.

As we kids got older and started our own families, it grew harder for everyone to come together every Christmas—so my mom invented a new annual family holiday around Flag Day. She brought us all to her house for a weekend of barbecue, outside games—and a play she'd write for the grandchildren. Every year, a month or two before Flag Day, she'd send out the scripts and casting assignments. She'd put together costumes, and when we all came together, the grandkids would rehearse under her direction before putting on their grand performance for the family.

I'm telling you this in part to celebrate my mother, a lively, fun, and artistic woman, but also because everyone we love has a story. When that person is taken from us by death or changed forever by injury, we don't want to lose who they were. We don't want them to die for nothing. We don't want the beauty they brought to this earth to disappear.

It's not about bringing them back, though surely we would if we could; it's about ensuring that their lives mattered and are remembered.

We can't control what happens in life, but we can control what we do next. That's why it's natural—and important—to find meaning in your loss.

In part, that's a matter of seeking accountability. How can you prevent what happened to your loved one from happening to someone else?

It's also a matter of remembrance and trying to serve others in their memory, in ways big or small.

In going through my mother's effects, we came across a box in a closet that contained her master's thesis, written on a typewriter back in 1977. She'd also taken pieces from the sets of productions she directed and turned them into art pieces on display in her house. All artifacts of her life journey.

Those discoveries led my wife to first reach out to the University of Florida's fine arts department to discuss two things:

1. Helping real people in real time who are going to school there now and who are trailblazers in their own ways, through a partial scholarship or grant in mom's name.

2. Displaying some of my mom's artifacts, permanently, as a testament to the trailblazer she was.

As I'm writing this book our entire extended family has come together on this project and we are in final discussions with the University of Florida to make this a reality. We're extremely excited about the prospect of meeting with future recipients of the financial assistance awarded in her name. Does it bring my mother back? No. But it carries her, and her story, forward in a way that helps others who are pursuing the same dreams she did.

SIGNS AND RITUALS OF REMEMBRANCE

We found a collection of T-shirts in my mother's closet—shirts with signs and slogans, positive expressions, that we'd all seen her wearing at one time or another. Keepsakes from races she'd run and other expressions of her passions and her personality.

My wife gathered these T-shirts and had them made into three quilts. One for each of our children. They're not big enough to keep anyone warm in winter, but they're Big Sissy's T-shirts, there for each of them to have and hold and cherish.

Back in Chapter 1, I wrote about a second form of keepsake, available only for the briefest of times: a fingerprint, taken before my mother's cremation and preserved in pendants for our children.

Small things. But keepsakes are one form of remembrance that can carry a loved one forward, with consequences well beyond their size.

I've met families who have planted trees in honor of their loved one or created memorial gardens, living things that they can visit and that others can enjoy. My mother's sister did just that, in a fairly secluded area of her yard away from the street and outside activity. She goes there to meditate next to the roses, succulents, and a "tree of life spinner," among the other plants and memorial items placed there. Others might place a bench in a location their loved one cherished, dedicated to their memory, or a roadside cross or sign marking the spot where they died—a form of remembrance and, perhaps, deterrence in hopes of saving others. If you honor a loved one by dedicating a pew in church, there's a closeness that occurs every time you go to church and slide into that pew with your family.

One family who lost a loved one to a drunk driver created an annual golf tournament in his memory. Their family member had loved golf, and they memorialized his passion in a fundraiser whose proceeds support others who have been victimized by drunk drivers. Does it raise a ton of money? It doesn't have to. To me, that's a perfect example of bringing accountability, remembrance, and serving your loved one's memory together.

Others might start a new tradition. I came across an example on the website Caring Bridge in which someone wrote of their late mother's love of cooking. They gathered and distributed her recipes to family members, who agreed to pick and prepare a favorite on Mother's Day each year, when they'd all come together to share in a meal rich in meaning and remembrance.

TAKING ACTION

There's a reason the victim's rights laws enacted around the country are commonly—and often officially—known as Marsy's Law. As I discussed in Chapter 3, it's because her family was determined that other families who endured a traumatic loss would not be victimized a second time by the criminal justice process itself.

You see it all the time. A family suffers a horrible loss under a particular circumstance. They see a need for reform. And they set out to advocate for change in the legislature, in the name of their loved one, in the hope of helping others. I don't mean to be political, but it could be a death at the hands of the police or a shooting in a school or a nightclub. It could be as simple as petitioning for a stop sign at a bad intersection or a lower speed limit on a bad stretch of road.

Having endured a tragic loss, you might now understand the depths of their motivation—both to honor the person they've lost and to regain some sense of control by trying to make something good, however small, out of something awful and to honor the memory of their loved one by doing it in their name.

Advocacy isn't for everyone, and you shouldn't feel you're failing your loved one if it's a path you don't choose. For you, it might be as simple as smiling at the shoppers you encounter in the grocery store and saying, "I hope your day is okay." For others, it might be taking the world by the tail and shaking it hard.

The point I'm making is that all of these are ways of honoring the legacy of the person you've lost by touching others in a positive way.

MORE THAN ANOTHER STATISTIC

For my family, seeking help to understand and process our feelings of grief has been an important element in regaining some sense of control over the uncontrollable. So has finding ways to remember and honor the woman we all loved as Big Sissy.

There's no fixing the tragedy that claimed her life. But we don't want her to be reduced to another number in the table of pedestrians killed in the state of Florida in 2020. My mother wasn't a footnote. She wasn't a statistic. Your loved one wasn't either. And there are ways—healthy ways, important both in looking back and moving forward, for your family and for others—to ensure that they're never reduced to just another number.

Conclusion

This is a book I hope you never *have* to read. But if you do, I hope it provides you with answers you need to the very difficult and important questions that begin to swirl around you immediately following the traumatic death or catastrophic injury of someone you love.

It will happen time and again: This just came up. What do I do?

I know, because it happened to me and my family. As a personal injury lawyer, I had been representing others who endured the unthinkable loss or injury of a loved one for more than twenty-five years. For them, in one moment, life seemed good; in the next, chaos. Yet all that experience didn't fully prepare me for my own immersion in tragedy.

When the unthinkable befell my family on the day my mother was struck and killed by a concrete mixer truck, I was stunned by the speed at which we were compelled to make important decisions. Many of them had lasting consequences, beginning with our ability to understand what happened and hold those responsible accountable for our loss. All my years of legal work were certainly helpful, but far from enough.

No one should be put in a position of making decisions this important in the dark.

As we emerged from the shock and upheaval of my mother's death, I realized that I was in a very real position to help. I have decades of professional experience helping families like yours, and now, mine has gotten that life-changing knock on the door just like yours too.

More than a year after we got that knock on the door, we continue moving forward one day at a time. All of us remember my mother in ways big and small. We are looking forward to establishing a scholarship in her name. We have been successful in bringing safety changes to hundreds of concrete mixer trucks, including the truck that took her life. In the year of the COVID-19 pandemic, we came together safely as a family to celebrate her life.

We miss Big Sissy dearly. We wish every day that she was still with us. But she's not. That we can't change.

You may know how that feels.

I think of this book as a way of honoring my mother. If not for her death, I wouldn't have seen the importance of writing it and sharing what I know. For me, this is one aspect of her legacy, of paying forward all that she meant to me.

I'm not here to tell you what you should do in the face of tragedy. The choices are yours to make. My goal has been to provide you with the information you need to make those choices. My heart is with you, and I hope this book helps.

Victim's Rights Laws

If a state has provided crime victims with rights under their state constitution, I have noted the section where the rights are specified below. To read what your state's constitution says, do an online search for the state name along with the word "constitution" and the article number listed below.

Whether they provide constitutional protections or not, most states have enacted laws that detail the rights of crime victims. These laws are listed below too. Again, to read your state law, do an online search for the state name and the statute number I've provided. (You can also find the same list with clickable links to the actual laws on my website, *KyleBachus.com*.)

ALABAMA

- Constitutional Protection: Article I, Section 6.01
- Victim's Rights Laws:
    - Ala. Code Section 15-23-60-84
      (The Crime Victims' Bill of Rights)
    - Ala. Code Section 15-14-53

ALASKA

- Constitutional Protection: Article I, Section 24
- Victim's Rights Laws:
  - Alaska Stat. Section 12.61.010-900
  - Alaska Stat. Section 12.55.011

ARIZONA

- Constitutional Protection: Article 2, Section 2.1
- Victim's Rights Law: A.R.S 13-4401-4441

ARKANSAS

- Constitutional Protection: None
- Victim's Rights Laws:
  - Ark. Code Ann. Section 16-90-1101-1115 (Rights of Victims of Crime)
  - Ark. Code Ann. Section 16-90-301-308 (Restitution to Victims)
  - Ark. Code Ann. Section 16-21-106 (Victim's Right to be Noticed)
  - Ark Code Ann. Section 16-90-701-719 (Victims Rights)

CALIFORNIA

- Constitutional Protection: California Constitution Article 1, Section 28
- Victim's Rights Laws:
  - California Penal Code Section 679-680 (Rights of Victims)

- ○ California Penal Code 1102.6
  (Right to be Present at Proceedings)

COLORADO

- Constitutional Protection: Colorado Constitution
  Article II, Section 16a
- Victim's Rights Laws:
  - ○ C.R.S Section 24-4.1-108
  - ○ C.R.S Section 24-4.1-301-304

CONNECTICUT

- Constitutional Protection: Connecticut Constitution
  Article I, Section 8b
- Victim's Rights Law: C.G.S Section 54-201-230

DELAWARE

- Constitutional Protection: None
- Victim's Rights Law: Delaware Code Section
  9401-9420

FLORIDA

- Constitutional Protection: Florida Constitution
  Article I, Section 16(b)
- Victim's Rights Law: F.S. Section 960.001

GEORGIA

- Constitutional Protection: Georgia Constitution Art. I,
  Section I, Paragraph XXX
- Victim's Rights Law: O.C.G.A Section 17-17-1-16

HAWAII

- Constitutional Protection: None
- Victim's Rights Law: Hawaii Revised Statutes Section 801D-1-7

IDAHO

- Constitutional Protection: Idaho Constitution Article 1, Section 22
- Victim's Rights Law: Idaho Code Section 19-5302-5306

ILLINOIS

- Constitutional Protection: Illinois Constitution Article I, Section 8.1 (Marsy's Law)
- Victim's Rights Laws: ILCS Chapter 725, Act 120/1-9

INDIANA

- Constitutional Protection: Indiana Constitution Article I, Section 13(b)
- Victim's Rights Law: I.C Section 35-40-5-(1-11)

IOWA

- Constitutional Protection: None
- Victim's Rights Law: I.C. Section 915.1-94

KANSAS

- Constitutional Protection: Kansas Constitution Article XV, Section 15
- Victim's Rights Law: K.S.A Section 74-7333-7338

KENTUCKY

- Constitutional Protection: Kentucky Constitution Amendment 1 (Marsy's Law)
- Victim's Rights Law: K.R.S Section 421.500-576

LOUISIANA

- Constitutional Protection: Louisiana Constitution Article I, Section 25
- Victim's Rights Law: L.R.S. 46 Section 1841

MAINE

- Constitutional Protection: None
- Victim's Rights Laws:
  - M.R.S 15 Section 6101
  - M.R.S 17 Section 1171-1177

MARYLAND

- Constitutional Protection: Maryland Constituion Article XLVII
- Victim's Rights Laws:
  - MD Crim Pro Code Section 6-106
  - MD Crim Pro Code Section 7-105
  - MD Crim Pro Code Section 11-101

MASSACHUSETTS

- Constitutional Protection: None
- Victim's Rights Law: M.G.L. c. 258B Section 1-13

MICHIGAN

- Constitutional Protection: Michigan Constitution Article I, Section 24
- Victim's Rights Law: M.R.S 780.751-834

MINNESOTA

- Constitutional Protection: None
- Victim's Rights Law: Minn. Stat. Section 611A.01-06

MISSISSIPPI

- Constitutional Protection: Mississippi Constitution Article III, Section 26A
- Victim's Rights Law: MS. Code Section 99-43-1-49

MISSOURI

- Constitutional Protection: Missouri Constitution Article I, Section 32
- Victim's Rights Law: R.S.M.O Section 595-200-218

MONTANA

- Constitutional Protection: Montana Constitution Article II, Section 28
- Victim's Rights Law: M.C.A Section 46-24-101-213

NEBRASKA

- Constitutional Protection: Nebraska Constitution Article I, Section 28
- Victim's Rights Law: N.R.S Section 81-1843-1851

NEVADA

- Constitutional Protection: Nevada Constitution Article II, Section 8A
- Victim's Rights Laws:
  - N.R.S. 14 Section 176.015
  - N.R.S. 14 Section 176A.630

NEW HAMPSHIRE

- Constitutional Protection: None
- Victim's Rights Laws:
  - N.H. Rev. Stat. Section 21-M:8-k
  - N.H. Rev. Stat. Section 21-M:8-c

NEW JERSEY

- Constitutional Protection: New Jersey Constitution Article I, Section 22
- Victim's Rights Laws: N.J.S.A Section 52:4B-34-44

NEW MEXICO

- Constitutional Protection: New Mexico Constitution Article II, Section 24
- Victim's Rights Law: N.M.S.A Section 31-26-1-16

NEW YORK

- Constitutional Protection: None
- Victim's Rights Law: NY Exec L Section 640-649

NORTH CAROLINA

- Constitutional Protection: North Carolina Constitution Article I, Section 37
- Victim's Rights Law: NC Gen Stat Section 15A-824-841

NORTH DAKOTA

- Constitutional Protection: North Dakota Constitution Article I, Section 25
- Victim's Rights Laws:
  - N.D.C.C. Section 12.1-34-01-05
  - N.D.C.C. Section 12.1-35-01-06

OHIO

- Constitutional Protection: Ohio Constitution Article I, Section 10a
- Victim's Rights Law: Ohio Rev. Code Section 2930.01-19

OKLAHOMA

- Constitutional Protection: Oklahoma Constitution Article II, Section 34
- Victim's Rights Laws:
  - Okla. Stat. Section 142A-B
  - Okla. Stat Section 40.1-3

OREGON

- Constitutional Protection: Oregon Constitution Article I, Section 42–43

- Victim's Rights Law: O.R.S Section 147.405-421

PENNSYLVANIA

- Constitutional Protection: None
- Victim's Rights Law: 18 Pa C.S. Section 11.101-502

RHODE ISLAND

- Constitutional Protection: Rhode Island Constitution Article I, Section 23
- Victim's Rights Law: RI Gen. Laws. Section 12-28-1-13

SOUTH CAROLINA

- Constitutional Protection: South Carolina Constitution Article I, Section 24
- Victim's Rights Law: S.C. Code. Ann. Section 16-3-1505

SOUTH DAKOTA

- Constitutional Protection: South Dakota Constitution Article VI, Section 29
- Victim's Rights Law: SDCL Section 23A-28C-1-9

TENNESSEE

- Constitutional Protection: Tennessee Constitution Article I, Section 35
- Victims Rights Law: Tenn. Code Ann. Section 40-38-101-302

TEXAS

- Constitutional Protection: Texas Constitution Article I, Section 30
- Victim's Rights Law: Texas Code of Crim. Procedure Section 56.01-15

UTAH

- Constitutional Protection: Utah Constitution Article I, Section 28
- Victim's Rights Laws:
  - Utah Code of Criminal Procedure Section 77-38-1-14
  - Utah Code of Criminal Procedure Section 77-37-1-5

VERMONT

- Constitutional Protection: None
- Victims Rights Law: 13 V.S.A. 5301-5322

VIRGINIA

- Constitutional Protection: Virginia Constitution Article I, Section 8-A
- Victim's Rights Laws:
  - Va. Code Ann. Section 16.1-302.1
  - Va. Code Ann. Section 19.2-11.01-11.4

WASHINGTON

- Constitutional Protection: Washington Constitution Article I, Section 35
- Victim's Rights Law: R.C.W. Section 7.69.010-7.69B.050

WASHINGTON, D.C.

- Constitutional Protection: None (not a state, so no state constitution)
- Victim's Rights Law: D.C. Code Section 23-1901-1911

WEST VIRGINIA

- Constitutional Protection: None
- Victim's Rights Laws:
  - W. Va. Code Section 61-11A-1-8
  - W. Va. Code Section 14-2A-1-29

WISCONSIN

- Constitutional Protection: Wisconsin Constitution Article I, Section 9m
- Victim's Right Law: Wis. Stat. Section 950.01-11

WYOMING

- Constitutional Protection: None
- Victim's Rights Laws:
  - Wy. Stat. Section 7-21-101-103
  - Wy. Stat. Section 14-6-501-509

Letter to Prosecutor's Office

Your letter should be sent by certified mail, and this is the text that should follow:

District Attorney's Office (and address)

Re: Wrongful Death Claim of (victim's name)
     Offender Name:
     Date of Loss:
     Date of Birth:

Dear District Attorney:

Thank you for your investigation and continued work in prosecuting this matter. Please be advised that I have been retained to serve as legal counsel to the family of (victim's name). On behalf of the victim's family, please know that the family is very grateful for your valuable and skilled services. I am writing at this time to formally request the records, information, and victim notifications available through your agency to crime victims under (the state where the case is being tried and the name and section number of its victim's rights law, as found in Appendix 1).

Please promptly provide the following information and/or notifications:

- Written information regarding victims' rights.
- Decisions made regarding the filing of felony charges and an explanation of charges filed.
- Decisions made regarding the filing of lower charges than the charge for which the person was initially arrested and whether the lower charge may result in a lower bond.
- Information regarding the internal file number assigned by your office to the case along with the name, address, and phone number of the deputy district attorney and of the courtroom to which the case is assigned.
- Advance written notice of the date, time, and place of every critical stage in the case and the opportunity to be present and, where appropriate, heard in court.
- Notification of any pending motions that may substantially delay your prosecution.
- The opportunity to consult with the family regarding any reduction of charges, negotiated pleas, diversion, or dismissal.
- Information regarding the function of the Pre-Sentence Report, the name and phone number of the probation office preparing the report, and the right to make a victim impact statement.

- Information regarding the option to use a form provided by your office to make a victim statement and
  information regarding policies giving the defendant a
  right to view the victim impact statement and information regarding the process by which the family will be
  given the ability to be present and heard orally and/or
  in writing at sentencing.

- Provide the family with the opportunity to speak with
  the prosecutor before the case is resolved and to be
  informed of the resolution.

- Provide the family's information to the court to ensure
  the family's participation in restitution proceedings
  along with an explanation of what is recoverable.

- Inform the family of the availability of: support
  available for crime victims and their immediate family
  members, including transportation to court; financial
  assistance; referral to community services; childcare,
  elder care, and disabled assistance; intercession with
  creditors and employers; translation services; and
  address protection.

- Inform the family on what to do in case of intimidation or harassment by the suspect and provide information about protection services including victim address
  confidentiality.

- Keep the family informed of when the offender is
  released from custody, permanently transferred from a
  county jail, is paroled, or escapes.

- Allow the family to view all or a portion of the
  pre-sentence report from the probation department.

- Ensure that the family receives a free copy of the initial
  incident report.

Regarding the critical stages of the criminal case please keep the family fully updated regarding the following events during the prosecution:

- The filing of charges, or decision not to file charges
- The preliminary hearing
- The arraignment of a person accused of a crime
- Any hearing on motions concerning evidentiary matters or pre- or post-plea relief
- Any disposition of the complaint or charges against the person accused
- The trial
- Any sentencing hearing or re-sentencing hearing
- Any attack on a judgment or conviction
- Any hearing regarding a reopened case due to lost or destroyed evidence
- The filing of any complaint, summons, or warrant by the probation department for failure to report to probation or because the location of a person convicted of a crime is unknown
- The decision to enter into a diversion agreement

We are very grateful for your cooperation in keeping us informed of the status of prosecutorial work in this matter. If we can assist you or your investigation in any way, or if you have any questions or concerns, please contact my paralegal (name and contact information), and we will set a call with the members of our team handling this matter.

Thank you in advance for your professional assistance.

Entry of Appearance

(Name, address, and phone number of court where the case is being heard)

People of the state of (state where the case is being tried) v. (the defendant's name)

Case number: (put the case number here)

(Family spokesman's or lawyer's name and contact information)

(Your family spokesman's or lawyer's name) hereby enters an appearance on behalf of the family of (your loved one's name), the crime victim in this case. The family wishes to be heard in this matter.

In accordance with the mandatory requirements of (insert your state's victims rights law or laws) and the rights afforded therein, the victim in this matter formally makes the following requests:

1. To be informed of and to be present for all "critical stages" of the criminal justice process, including but not limited to the following stages:

   a. The filing of charges or decision not to file charges

   b. The arraignment

   c. Any hearing on motions concerning evidentiary matters or pre- or post-plea relief

   d. Any disposition of the complaint or charges

   e. The trial

   f. Any sentencing hearing

   g. Any appellate review or appellate decision

   h. Any attack on judgment or conviction

   i. The decision to enter into a diversion or other agreement

   j. To be notified in writing of all victim's rights

   k. To be informed of the status of the case and any scheduling changes or cancellations

2. To be free from intimidation, harassment, or abuse; to be told what steps to take if such events occur; and to be informed about available protection services.

3. To be informed when the offender is released from custody.

4. To be present and heard in court regarding any bond reduction or modification, acceptance of any nolo contendere plea or negotiated plea, sentencing, or any modification of a sentence.

5. To talk with the prosecutor before the case is resolved and to be informed of resolution.

6. To view the pre-sentence report.

7. To be afforded the opportunity to prepare a victim's impact statement and to be present and heard either orally and/or in writing (at the victim's selection) at sentencing.

8. To be afforded a hearing to determine the amount of restitution to be paid to the victim for all actual pecuniary damages.

9. To have the victim's written or oral impact statement included with any referral of the offender to community corrections.

10. To be afforded all other victim's rights available under (state where case is being tried) law.

Respectfully submitted this (month and day) of (year).

Letters to Corrections and Probation

(Title and address of the agency)

Re: Wrongful Death Claim of (your loved one's name) against (the offender's name and date of birth)

Dear Sir/Madam:

Thank you for your continued work on this matter. On behalf of the victim's family, please know that the family is very grateful for your valuable and skilled services. I am writing at this time to formally request the records, information, and victim notifications available through your agency to crime victims under (insert the state where the agency is located) Victim's Rights Act.

Please promptly provide us the following in writing regarding the subject offender:

- Notify the family of the institution where the offender is incarcerated.

- Notify the family of the offender's escape, transfer, or release from any state hospital or corrections facility.

- Notify the family in advance of transfer to or placement in a non-secure facility, from confinement, or discharge from incarceration, as well any conditions of release.

- Notify the family of the transition of the offender from a residential facility to a non-residential setting.

- Notify the family of parole hearings and full parole board reviews.

- Notify the family of any decision by the parole board or any decision by the governor to commute an offender's sentence or pardon the offender, prior to public disclosure.

- Notify the family of the death of the offender while confined.

- Notify the family of any discharge from parole.

We are very grateful for your cooperation in keeping us informed of the status of the offender. If you have any questions or concerns, please contact me at (family spokesperson's phone number).

Thank you in advance for your professional assistance.

Social Media Policies When Someone Dies

If a loved one has passed away, you may wonder what should be done about their social media accounts. If you have your loved one's account information, deleting accounts is usually as simple as logging on. If you do not have your loved one's account information, the information below may be helpful. This information is current as of 2021.

(You can find the same list with clickable links to the policies of these platforms on my website, *KyleBachus.com*.)

FACEBOOK/INSTAGRAM

If you do not know the Facebook password of your loved one's account, Facebook will not provide that password to you.

If you are a relative or close friend of an account holder, you have two options. (The same options can be taken for Instagram.)

You can ask Facebook to memorialize an account. (Do an online search for "Facebook" or "Instagram" and "when someone dies.") Depending on the settings you choose, your loved one's friends can still post remembrances or anecdotes on the page. The photos that your loved one shared are preserved, and nobody will be able to log into the account. The account will not appear in public search spaces.

If you are an immediate relative of your loved one, you can request that their account be removed entirely. To do this, you will need proof of authority including a power of attorney, birth certificate, last will and testament, or estate letter. You must also show proof of death using an obituary or memorial card.

TWITTER

Twitter does not distribute passwords to anyone regardless of relationship. You may only deactivate an account, not control it. This requires filling in an online form (do a search for "Twitter deactivating account") and providing the user's username, your name, your relationship with the account holder, your email, and additional information that could be helpful. Twitter will contact you if they require more information.

SNAPCHAT

Snapchat only allows one action when a user passes away: account deletion. Do an online search for "Snapchat support" and select the appropriate button. You will be required to provide a copy of the death certificate.

LINKEDIN

Like Facebook, LinkedIn will not distribute a deceased member's password; however, they will memorialize or close an account if you have the authority to act on behalf of your loved one.

If you memorialize the account, it will remain online, and content will not be deleted. The account will be tagged "in remembrance," and nobody will be able to log on. To memorialize an account, you must be able to provide the member's full name, their LinkedIn profile link, your relationship, the member's email address, the date of the member's passing, a copy of the member's death certificate, and a legal document showing you have the authority to act on behalf of a member. These include letters of administration, letters of testamentary, letters of representation, or another court order declaring you the representative of the estate. You must follow the same process to delete an account.

Do an online search for "LinkedIn when someone dies" for the link.

PINTEREST

Pinterest does not distribute passwords to any family member or loved one. They also do not publish specific policies on account closure but will close an account if your loved one has died. Do an online search for "Pinterest when someone dies" for the link, then provide your name, the name of the user, their username, their email address, and as much information about your relationship with your loved one as possible.

GOOGLE ACCOUNTS (YOUTUBE, GMAIL, ETC.)

First, check to see if your loved one has an "inactive account manager" set up on his or her account. If they do, this will give information about who your loved one has given permission to access the account information and content.

In other cases, Google only allows for the closing of the account of a deceased user. Do an online search for "Google account when someone dies" for the link. You will need your loved one's name and email, your name and email, your government-issued ID, your loved one's death certificate, and any additional supporting documents you may have demonstrating representation.

Without the password, it is difficult for Google to provide any information such as actual emails or other personal information stored in Google Drive. Accessing this content is a lengthy process that generally requires a court order. If your loved one had a YouTube account that made money, you may also consider requesting those funds from Google's e-wallets (Wallet and AdSense). Do an online search for "Google submit a request regarding a deceased user's account."

TIKTOK

As of this writing, TikTok does not have a policy of deleting the accounts of those who have passed away. Unless you have the login information, you may not delete the account without cause. Currently, the death of a user is not a valid cause. That being said, if you have access to a loved one's mobile device, you may try opening the TikTok app. The app generally remains logged in, and if so, you can try to take the following steps to delete the account.

1. Go to **Me**.
2. Tap ... located on the top right corner.
3. Tap Manage account > Delete account.
4. Follow the instructions in the app to delete your account.

Additionally, if you have the proper legal authorization and access to a person's smartphone password, you can try to view saved internet passwords. If your loved one saved his or her Tik-Tok password, you may be able to access it, log into the account, and delete it.

REDDIT

Like TikTok, as of this writing, Reddit does not have a policy of deleting the accounts of those who are deceased. If you have access to your loved one's smartphone password, you can try to view saved passwords. If your loved one saved his or her Reddit password, you may be able to access it, log into the account, and delete it.

If you have the login information, do an online search for "delete Reddit account" and follow the steps, beginning with logging in if need be.

Intestate Succession Laws

To read what your state's intestate succession law actually says, do an online search for the state name along with the statute number I've provided. (You can also find the same list with clickable links to the actual laws on my website, *KyleBachus.com*.)

ALABAMA

Ala. Code Section 43-8-40 to 43-8-58

ALASKA

Alaska Statute Section 13.12.101 to 13.12.114

ARIZONA

Ariz. R.S. Section 14-2101 to 14-2114

ARKANSAS

Ark. Code Section 28-9-201 to 28-9-221

CALIFORNIA

Calif. Probate Section 6400 to 6455

COLORADO

Colo. Rev. St. Section 15-11-101 to 15-11-122

CONNECTICUT

Conn. Gen. St. Section 45a-273 to 45a-468m

DELAWARE

Del. Code Title 12 Section 501 to 511

DISTRICT OF COLUMBIA

DC Code Section 19-301 to 19-322

FLORIDA

Fla. St. Section 732-101 to 732-111

GEORGIA

Ga. Code Section 53-2-1 to 53-2-51

HAWAII

Hawaii Rev. St. Section 560:2-101 to 560:2-114

IDAHO

Idaho St. Section 15-2-101 to 15-2-114

ILLINOIS

Ill. St. Ch. 755 Section 5/2-1 to 5/2-9

INDIANA

Ind. Code Section 29-1-2-0.1 to 29-1-2-15

IOWA

Iowa Code Section 633.210 to 633.231

KANSAS

Kan. St. Section 59-501 to 59-514

KENTUCKY

Kent. Rev. St. Section 391.010 to 391.360

LOUISIANA

La. Civ. Code Title I, Art. 880 to 901

MAINE

Maine Rev. St. Title 18-A Section 2-101 to 2-114

MARYLAND

Maryland Code, Estate & Trusts Section 3-101 to 3-112

MASSACHUSETTS

Mass. Gen. Laws Ch. 190B, Section 2-101 to 2-114

MICHIGAN

Mich. Comp. Laws Section 700.2101 to 700.2114

MINNESOTA

Minn. St. Section 524.2-101 to 524.2-123

MISSISSIPPI

Miss. Code Section 91-1-1 to 9-1-31

MISSOURI

Missouri Rev. St. Section 474.010 to 474.155

MONTANA

Mont. Code Ann. Section 72-11-101 to 72-11-104

NEBRASKA

Neb. Rev. St. Section 30-2301 to 30-2312

NEVADA

Nev. Rev. St. Section 134.005 to 134.210

NEW HAMPSHIRE

N.H. St. Section 561:1 to 561:21

NEW JERSEY

N.J. 3B Section 5-1 to 5-14.1

NEW MEXICO

N.M. St. Section 45-2-101 to 45-2-122

NEW YORK

N.Y. Est. Pow. & Trust Section 4-1.1 to 4-1.6

NORTH CAROLINA

N.C. Gen. St. Section 29-1 to 29-30

NORTH DAKOTA

N.D. Cent. Code Section 30.1-04-01 to 30.1-04-21

OHIO

Ohio Rev. Code Section 2105.01 to 2105.39

OKLAHOMA

Okla. St. Section 84-4-211 to 84-4-232

OREGON

Ore. Rev. St. Section 112.015 to 112.115

PENNSYLVANIA

Penn. St. 20 Pa.C.S.A. Section 2101 to 2110

RHODE ISLAND

R.I. Gen. Laws Section 33-1-1 to 33-1-13

SOUTH CAROLINA

S.C. Code Section 62-2-101 to 62-2-114

SOUTH DAKOTA

S.D. Code Laws Ann. Section 29A-2-101 to 29A-2-114

TENNESSEE

Tenn. Code Section 31-2-101 to 31-2-110

TEXAS

Tex. Est. Section 201.001 to 201.003

UTAH

Utah Code Section 75-2-101 to 75-2-114

VERMONT

Vermont St. Title 14 Section 301 to 338

VIRGINIA

Virg. Code Section 64.2-200 to 64.2-206

WASHINGTON

Wash. Rev. Code Section 11.04.015 to 11.04.290

WEST VIRGINIA

W.V. Code Section 42-1-1 to 42-1-10

WISCONSIN

Wisc. St. Section 852.01 to 852.14

WYOMING

Wyo. St. Section 2-4-101 to 2-4-214

Small Estate Affidavit

This is drawn from the form for the state of Colorado and is intended to serve as a sample, giving you an idea what the affidavit might look like. In this case, the numbers and statute name are specific to Colorado. Different states have different rules and forms. You should be able to find the form for your state by doing an online search for your state name followed by the words "small estate affidavit."

I, (name), the affiant, am either a successor of the decedent or a person acting on behalf of one or more of the successors of the decedent, and I am eighteen years of age or older.

At least ten days have elapsed since the death of (loved one's name).

The total fair market value of all property owned by the decedent and subject to disposition by will or intestate succession at the time of the decedent's death, wherever that property is located, less liens and encumbrances, does not exceed, for year of death (Y.O.D.): Y.O.D. 2020 and 2021 is $70,000; Y.O.D. 2019 is

$68,000; Y.O.D. 2017 and 2018 is $66,000; Y.O.D. 2016, 2015, and 2014 is $64,000; and Y.O.D. 2013 is $63,000.

This affidavit is not valid for the transfer of real estate. To transfer personal property that affects real estate see Section 15-12-1201(3.5), C.R.S.

No application or petition for the appointment of a personal representative is pending or has been granted in any jurisdiction.

The successor(s), listed below, is/are entitled to any personal property belonging to the decedent, including but not limited to funds on deposit at, or any contents of, a safe deposit box at any financial institution; tangible personal property; or instrument evidencing a debt, obligation, stock chose in action (right to bring a legal action), or stock brand. The amount, proportion, or percentage that each successor is entitled to is as follows:

Name of Successor	Description of Property	Amount

1. The property must be paid or delivered as described in the following table, and then the property will be distributed to successors in accordance with paragraph 6 above:

Name of Successor or Person Collecting on Behalf of One or More Successors	Description of Property	Amount

2. Any person collecting property on behalf of one or more successors will be deemed an agent of such successor with all the duties of an agent under Colorado law.

3. I understand that any person who receives property pursuant to this affidavit is answerable and accountable to any subsequently appointed personal representative of the estate or any other person having a superior right to the estate.

VERIFICATION AND ACKNOWLEDGMENT

I, (name), swear/affirm under oath that I have read the foregoing COLLECTION OF PERSONAL PROPERTY BY AFFI-DAVIT PURSUANT TO Section 15-12-1201, C.R.S. and that the statements set forth therein are true and correct to the best of my knowledge.

(Here you'd print your name. Sign and date in the presence of a notary, who would verify your identity.)

Wrongful Death Laws

To read what your state's wrongful death law actually says, do an online search for the state name along with the statute number I've provided. (You can also find the same list with clickable links to the actual laws on my website, *KyleBachus.com*.)

Remember: don't feel as if you have to hire a lawyer just to understand your state's law. While it may be a little wordy, you should be able to grasp what it means for bringing a wrongful death case in your state.

ALABAMA
Ala. Code Section 6-5-410

ALASKA
Alaska Stat. AS 09.55.580

ARIZONA
Ari. Rev. Section 12-611, 12-612, 12-613

ARKANSAS

Ark. Code Section 12-62-102

CALIFORNIA

Cal. Code of Civ. Proc. Section 377.60, 377.61

COLORADO

Colo. Rev. Stat. Section 13-21-201, 13-21-202 (2021)

CONNECTICUT

Conn. Gen. Stat. Section 52-555

DELAWARE

Del. Code Title 10 Section 3724

DISTRICT OF COLUMBIA

DC Code Section 16-2701, 16-2703

FLORIDA

Fla. Section 768.16-768.26

GEORGIA

Ga. Code Title 51 Torts Section 51-4-2

HAWAII

Hawaii Rev. Stat. Div. 4 Section 663-3

IDAHO

Idaho Stat. Title 5 Section 5-311

ILLINOIS

Ill. Stat. Chapter 740, Section 180

INDIANA

Indiana Code Section 34-23-1-1

IOWA

Iowa Code Title XV Section 633.336

KANSAS

Kan. Stat. Chapter 60 Section 60-1901

KENTUCKY

Kent. Revised Statutes Title XXXVI Section 411.130

LOUISIANA

La. Civil Code Tit. V, Art. 2315.2

MAINE

Maine Rev. Stat. Title 18-A Section 2-804

MARYLAND

Md. Code, Courts and Judicial Proceedings Section 3-904

MASSACHUSETTS

Mass. Gen. Laws Part III Ch. 229, Section 2

MICHIGAN

Michigan Comp. Laws, Chapter 600 Section 600.2922

MINNESOTA

Minn. Stat. Section 573.02

MISSISSIPPI

Miss. Code Title 11 Section 11-7-13

MISSOURI

Missouri Rev. Stat. Title XXXVI Section 537.080

MONTANA

Mont. Title 27 Section 27-1-513

NEBRASKA

Neb. Rev. Stat. Chapter 30 Section 30-809

NEVADA

Nev. Rev. Stat. Title 3 Section 41.085

NEW HAMPSHIRE

N.H. Rev. Stat. Title LVI Section 556:12

NEW JERSEY

N.J. Wrongful Death Act

NEW MEXICO

N.M. Stat. Section 41-2-1

NEW YORK

N.Y. Cons. Laws, Estates, Powers and Trusts Law Section 5-4.1

NORTH CAROLINA

N.C. Gen. Stat. Section 28A-18-2

NORTH DAKOTA

N.D. Cent. Code Section 32-21-01

OHIO

Ohio Rev. Code Title XXI Section 2125.01

OKLAHOMA

Okla. Stat. Section 12-1053

OREGON

Ore. Rev. Stat. Section 30.020

PENNSYLVANIA

Penn. Stat. Title 42 Pa.C.S.A. Judiciary and Judicial Procedure
Section 8301

RHODE ISLAND

R.I. Gen. Laws Section 10-7-1

SOUTH CAROLINA

S.C. Code of Laws Section 15-51-10

SOUTH DAKOTA

S.D. Cod. Laws Section 21-5-5

TENNESSEE

Tenn. Code Section 20-5-106

TEXAS

Tex. Civ. Prac. & Rem. Code Section 71.00

UTAH

Utah Code Section 78B-3-106

VERMONT

Vt. Stat. Title 14 Section 1491

VIRGINIA

Va. Code Section 8.01-50

WASHINGTON

Wash. Rev. Code Section 4.20.010

WEST VIRGINIA

W.V. Code Section 55-7-5

WISCONSIN

Wisc. Statutes Section 895.04

WYOMING

Wyo. Statutes Section 1-38-101

Acknowledgments

I want to start with a huge and heartfelt thank-you to my wife, Jessica, for being there for me and for putting up with our crazy schedule and the long hours over the last twenty-plus years—time spent in the pursuit of justice and accountability for so many families. Thank you for your love and support, for being my sounding board, and for your insight, input, and compassion. All while being a great mom to our children! Words cannot express the appreciation I have for all the things you did when tragedy struck our family on a random Tuesday night. You jumped into action the moment I walked upstairs with the horrible news: trying to console me and the kids in the midst of your own shock and grief, getting us on a plane to Florida, and going into Mom's house to rescue her cats and secure her laptop, Shutterfly, and email accounts when I wasn't ready to enter. And weeks later, being there with me sorting through Mom's belongings, along with the countless other things you have done since to help preserve her memory and legacy for our family. I love you very much.

Thank you to Bailey, Kamden, Karson, and our sweet angel Kenzi for all the love, support, inspiration, and perspective you have given to me since the day you were born. You are so loved,

and I couldn't be more proud of you! Thank you for letting me be
your dad. I am so very sorry that you lost your Big Sissy, but I am
also so very grateful for the time you spent with her. I know how
much Big Sissy cherished every moment of her time with you,
and I am thankful I was able to be there to see all the love. She
loved you so much and was so proud to be your grandmother.

To Darin Schanker, my law partner of more than twenty-five
years. Who would have thought back in 1996 that, twenty-five
years later, we would still be able to do this work together and
that our firm would grow to have the firepower, resources, and
legal talent it has today. Darin, I am forever indebted to you for
everything you did for me and my family from the moment I
reached out to tell you the news about my mom. You dropped
everything and took immediate action to help my family. You
had engineers and investigative boots on the ground in Florida
within twenty-four hours, which proved to be invaluable, while
my own head was spinning with grief. Just knowing that you
and a team of experts were working to preserve evidence and get
answers about what happened provided my entire family with
a measure of control in the chaos. You have sacrificed and have
been there every step of the way for me as a friend but also as
my family's lawyer. Thank you!

Thank you to Zachary Wool, Jessica Perez Reynolds, Maaren
Johnson, Lauren Epke, Edie Britton, Melanie Sulkin, and the
rest of the top-shelf legal team that quickly assembled to seek
answers, accountability, and justice for my mom. I know from
Darin that each one of you reached out and volunteered to work
on my mom's case despite your busy schedules. Thank you for
being amazing friends and for offering up your many talents on
behalf of my mom. I will never forget your kindness. You are all
such amazing people.

Edie, I also need to thank you for all you did to keep this book on schedule along with organizing the rest of my professional life during such a difficult year. The book would not have been completed when it was without you.

To Mark Travis. This book literally would not exist without you. I am so thankful that we had the opportunity to work together on it. I like to think that Big Sissy played a role in finding you; she was terrific at identifying talented people. Thank you for your guidance and commitment to the process. Thank you for the gentle and compassionate way you helped me work through the very difficult but important topics that had to be re-lived to make this book what it is. Thank you for helping me honor my mom. I also want to thank the rest of the Scribe publishing and editorial teams who were indispensable in making this book a reality.

To Aaron Evans. Thank you for the guidance you have provided over so many years to our clients on all things related to probate law, wills, trusts, and estate planning. You are a tremendous lawyer and an even better friend! Thank you for your willingness to share your legal expertise with me on this project.

To Bastion Kane, undoubtedly one of the top legal brief writers in the United States. Thank you for two decades of friendship and collaboration. Thank you for your outstanding work with the experts and your briefing on the many important legal issues involved in my mom's case. Thank you for always being there for my family.

Justin Ferrugia, thank you for the comprehensive research you provided on many of the important topics we covered in this book. Your work on this project will be very helpful to families throughout the country who are confronting traumatic loss.

Thank you to Laurie Meadows for working with me to process my grief and traumatic loss. It has been a long road. I am so thankful for your professional help. You are amazing at your job! And thank you to Elishia Oliva for your many years of friendship, for being there for my family in our time of crisis, and for suggesting I read Megan Devine's book. It changed my perspective and is really the impetus for my decision to write this book.

To my brother, Kirk, and sister, Kara. Thank you for being in my corner my whole life and for being there for me after we lost our mom.

Bonnye, Larry, and Sharri, thank you for a lifetime of being there for Big Sissy 100 percent of the time and for all you have done to honor her life! I know how much she loved each of you.

Mom, Dad, and Cindy, thank you for having my back forever and for the unconditional love and support you have always given to our entire family!

About the Author

Kyle Bachus won his first argument in front of the state supreme court when he was seventeen years old. As a junior in high school, Kyle attended a Florida state legislation day for high school students. There, he was selected to argue a predetermined topic in front of a panel of licensed lawyers sitting on a mock supreme court. He was provided with appropriate documentation and tasked with researching and preparing his argument. Selected as one of the best presenters of the day statewide, he was both surprised and inspired to pursue a career in law.

He graduated from the University of Florida with a Bachelor of Science degree in 1989 and from the University of Florida College of Law three years later. He began work the Monday after graduation in a plaintiff's personal injury law firm.

Kyle moved to Colorado in 1994 and joined a Denver personal injury law firm. Two years later, Kyle and fellow lawyer Darin Schanker opened Bachus & Schanker, LLC in a tiny, rented office with less than $15,000. In the years since, Bachus & Schanker has grown into one of the largest personal injury firms in the region. Today, Kyle oversees the firm's Elite Litigation Group, where he limits his personal practice to representing families throughout the United States in wrongful death and catastrophic injury cases.

Kyle is a member of the Colorado and Florida Bar associations and has served on the Board of Directors of the Colorado Trial Lawyers Association for more than twenty years in total. He has served on numerous committees and repeatedly won recognition from his peers at both the state and national level. He is proud of the role he has played in the passage of state and national legislation to protect consumers and is a frequent speaker and guest lecturer.

Kyle lives in Denver with his wife and their three children.